The Best of
No Small Thing

MINDFUL
MEDITATIONS

The Best of No Small Thing

MINDFUL MEDITATIONS

FAVORITE POSTS FROM 10 YEARS OF
POPULAR BLOG, *NOSMALLTHING.NET*

DEBORAH HAWKINS

Columbus, Ohio

The Best of No Small Thing – Mindful Meditations

Published by Gatekeeper Press
2167 Stringtown Rd, Suite 109
Columbus, OH 43123-2989
www.GatekeeperPress.com

Copyright © 2019 by Deborah Hawkins

All rights reserved. Neither this book, nor any parts within it may be sold or reproduced in any form or by any electronic or mechanical means, including information storage and retrieval systems without permission in writing from the author. The only exception is by a reviewer, who may quote short excerpts in a review.

ISBN (paperback): 9781642378528
eISBN: 9781642378535

Contents

A Few Words About This Collection

Nearly ten years ago, I started a blog to help me direct my thoughts in a positive way, specifically to things I was grateful for.

I was inspired by Eckhart Tolle's words, "Acknowledging the good that you already have in your life is the foundation for all abundance."

Observing events and people in my life with the intention of identifying the good already present became a regular, almost automatic, habit. I found myself bringing heightened awareness to notice small things that enriched my daily life.

A mindfulness approach to gratitude became a practice for me. Combining this orientation—to apply attention and reverence to observing my life—with the understanding that these moments needed to be charged with emotion in order to have the greatest impact, I started wrapping stories around moments where I recognized feeling grateful, and…

…**No Small Thing – Mindful Meditations** was born.

This collection of fifty favorite posts, written over the last ten years, are examples of my approach.

I have put together a companion book, **Practice Gratitude: Transform Your Life**, as a guide to this process that has been life-changing for me.

I hope you can use what I have learned to allow gratitude and mindfulness to elevate the way you see the world and yourself.

Good Advice

S INCE I STARTED writing down my mindful meditations, I have tried to pay extra attention to things that affect me, things that change my mood or outlook, or simply things that I'm grateful for. Keeping an eye out for these kinds of things has brought up memories of my father and some paradoxical advice he tried to impart.

My father died when he was sixty-two. I was in my mid-twenties and going through a divorce. He was not around often when I was growing up as he worked very long hours, but his presence was oh so constant. We didn't go to many ballgames together or to the park. He didn't teach me how to drive or mentor me in some important life skills, but I knew he loved me very much.

Starting when I was about thirteen, he used to pull me under his arm and repeat an odd phrase. "Don't worry about the little things. It's the big things that are important." Then he'd add, as if confiding something more profound to me, "Don't worry about *the big things*. It's *the little things* that are important."

So, what was he trying to tell me? What was I supposed to be wary of, I wondered, the BIG things or the LITTLE things? Was he simply telling me not to worry? What was I supposed to be getting out of this advice?

In a typical teenage way, I suppose, I dismissed his thought. *Must be on drugs*, I'd say to myself. This had become my catchall phrase whenever someone spoke or acted in ways I couldn't understand.

Throughout my life, I've had an uncomfortable reaction to getting advice I didn't know what to do with. My mother, for instance, who is now eighty-eight, likes to dispense recommendations automatically like a two-a-day standing order for Advil. Her directives often feel like criticisms and could range in topic from how I should style my hair to what route I should take driving her on errands.

Generally, I remember that the unsolicited opinions or advice she gives are more about her than about me. But still, I bristle when my mother, or a friend, or co-worker, or coach for that matter, feels compelled to give advice that has little to do with who I am and what I value.

Advice can often seem contradictory, hard to follow, or not true for me and my life.

Then I'll remember to look beyond the words and focus on the vibration of someone's counsel. I think about my father's love floating on top of his paradox, and I'm okay with whatever sentiment is expressed.

Accepting *the gift* of someone's advice without feeling compelled to take it is no small thing.

Grateful Dozen Category: People Who Touch Me,
August 5, 2010

Giving Yourself Permission

ON WEEKEND MORNINGS, I like to pick up a Take-a-Hike scone at the *Bleeding Heart Bakery* and walk over to Fellger Park and eat it slowly.

Fellger Park is a small park, size-wise, but I see it more as an incredible, magical play lot. It's equipped with benches for parents and nannies; swings, slides, small tables for make-believe tea parties, a red locomotive that doesn't go anywhere (ah, but I imagine sitting in it affords the greatest views), and a tree-shaped sprinkler that can cool down any munchkin during a summer heat wave.

The ground is also made out of that wonderful spongy material that seems to forgive falls and the effects that too much enthusiasm can have on a kid's skin.

Last Saturday, while sitting on one of the park's benches, I overheard a sweetly intimate father-daughter conversation. A three-year-old blonde girl, frail build, wearing glasses, was looking very circumspect at the fountain tree and the gleeful scurrying other kids made directly in the path of the water.

"Dad," she asked. "Can I go in?"

"Yes," he answered.

She didn't move. She just watched the other kids more intently.

"Dad," she repeated. "Can I go in?"

Her cheeks were tender and pink, like the insides of a bunny's ear.

"Yes," he repeated.

She thought quietly for a bit then posed the question differently:

"Dad, will you go in with me?"

"I didn't bring my bathing suit," he replied. "So I won't go in, but you can go in." He squeezed her hand and tried to reassure her. "You can go in."

She stood still for a while. A four-year-old boy, stripped down to his underpants, raced around, screaming by her, wet strands of his hair plastered against his freckles. He beat a circular path under and around the fountain. Then the coast was clear again.

I think she was about to ask her father yet one more time,

but instead took a sigh and walked slowly to the edge of the puddle made by the cascading water.

She didn't run underneath the stream. She raised one foot, white gym shoes still tied pristinely, and stamped it down with all her might, making the water splash upward, droplets of spray tickling her legs up to the hem of her shorts.

For now, this was enough. Maybe next week, she'll run her hands under the waterfall or step in barefoot. I was so proud of her.

Giving yourself permission to get wet is no small thing.

Grateful Dozen Category: Surprise,
July 14, 2010

The Same Everywhere

THE OTHER WEEK, I went on a long anticipated travel adventure with a friend.

I've been a big fan of Cajun and Zydeco music for years. At a Redstick Ramblers concert last year in Chicago, Kevin, the lead fiddler—a red-bearded gentle bear of a man—invited the entire audience to come down to Lahf-yet Looz-ee-anna for the Blackpot Festival and Gumbo Cook-off.

I plastered the last weekend of October dates all over my office as inspiration. When I accepted the fact that I would not be visiting South America this fall, there was no way I was going to miss the Blackpot Festival.

My friend and I flew down to the Big Easy Thursday, October 28th. The plan was to hang out in the French Quarter and warehouse district that day then pick up a car to drive to Lafayette on Friday morning. We'd leave Lafayette Sunday morning and drive back to N'awlins on Halloween, in time for brunch at Commander's Palace in the Garden District and then catch a small voodoo festival on Dumaine Street around sunset.

The minute I walked off the plane I was excited. I have a very special fondness for New Orleans, a town with more soul than any I can imagine. Ah, what to do first . . . There were plenty of antique shops and museums. I had never been to City Park before.

Weeks ago, I contemplated going on some type of cemetery and haunted house tour. But after we made an important lunch stop at Acme Oyster House for oyster po' boy sandwiches and Abita Amber, all we wanted to do was **BE** in New Orleans.

We simply walked around the Quarter, in and out of shops and art galleries, trying to jog our respective memories on past New Orleans adventures and remember our local geography. Was *The Kitchen Witch* where we thought it would be? Did St. Ann Street cut over all the way to Decatur Street? What was the best route to the Café du Monde?

Being in a new place with no particular destination is a joy. My friend and I exercised the simplest form of democracy.

After we looked into the windows of specialty stores and galleries, we would look up at each other with unattached openness. We didn't have to ask out loud. We negotiated the "Do you want to go in?" question by expression alone, one door at a time.

It seemed that the local school children were given the afternoon off to trick 'r treat among the small shops in the Quarter. The spirit of surprise and generosity was everywhere.

I saw fairy princesses and Darth Vaders, hobos and

bumblebees, skeletons, and knights in shining aluminum. The shopkeepers would comment appropriately on how beautiful or frightful their visitors were and dole out handfuls of candy from their waiting supply.

I thought about how a similar ritual was taking place on North Lincoln Avenue and Roscoe Street in my own neighborhood. The business owners would be finding the appeal of costumed children as enjoyable as ringing up their registers.

And I couldn't help but recall the adage about people being the same everywhere. This, of course, is true. Thing is, when I travel, ***I'm not the same.***

Traveling makes you look at things in a fresh way. It's a chance to see how people celebrate different traditions and demonstrate how they belong to their tribe. It's also a chance to ***see without looking.***

When you're out of your own routine and have no agenda or place where you have to be, you can really settle into the being-ness of where you are.

Appreciating the way a little trip opens your eyes and heart is no small thing.

Grateful Dozen Category: Belonging, Tourist Eyes,
November 8, 2010

Market Days

I LOVE GREEN CITY Market.

From May 12th through October 30th on Wednesdays and Saturdays, farmers from Indiana, Michigan, and Illinois set up tents and stands at the south side of Lincoln Park, appropriately perhaps, not far from the miniature farm in the zoo.

It's quite a festive, family-friendly atmosphere. Often, there are folding chairs set up so shoppers can listen to musicians.

Dogs on leashes and toddlers in their buggies visit the different kiosks under the watchful eyes of their owners and parents, the organic foodies high on the air of sustainability and pesticide-free produce.

The green beans are so fresh, they even taste good raw. Flaming Furies®, a name I've always thought more suitable for a ladies' softball team, and about a dozen other varieties of peaches are chin-dripping treats.

I used to think purple peppers were simply part of a tongue twister (Remember Peter picked a peck?) until I found some at the market.

There's a tent I visit regularly where they sell microgreens. They look like fine, colorful grasses, but are dense and loaded with flavors you would normally find in a milder form as some other vegetables like beets or radish.

There's a rainbow of apples, from red to pink to yellow to green. They're perfectly imperfect, of all different sizes, completely unselfconscious about a brown spot here or there. They know they are wonderfully crisp and not too sweet or too tart.

A red cabbage at Green City Market opens up like a corsage on homecoming, and the blueberry-raspberry-melon smoothies blended on site (where they plug in the blender, I don't know), you can't believe how good they are.

In June, the market has several vendors that sell wild prairie flowers. Asparagus is also plentiful. In July, you're more likely to see molded cardboard buckets of berries; red, blue, and black. And later in the summer, you'll start to see corn come in.

My fellow urbanites will pull back the husk from one or two ears before buying a bunch. I'm not sure that most of us really know the signs of a high-quality ear, but this seems to be everyone's routine. There's more corn in August and enough tomatoes to make Mama Ragu cry with joy. Now that it's September, I'm starting to see beets and a wider variety of peppers.

Don't get me wrong, I do appreciate that I can go to a nearby grocery store and find avocados year-round and can pretty much whip up a batch of guacamole anytime I want. Still, the fact that what I see any Wednesday or Saturday morning at Green City Market might not be there the following week makes me feel a special kind of appreciation.

Golden sunflowers or purple asparagus, bunches of basil or strawberries ready to be encrusted in dark chocolate: these things might only be available for a couple of weeks.

Enjoying things in *their season* is no small thing.

Grateful Dozen Category: Neighborhood Discoveries,
September 6, 2010

Night at the Lesbian Karoke Irish Bar

L AST SATURDAY, I asked a friend if she would go to a neighborhood street festival with me. It would be full of fun music, overpriced beer in plastic cups, great tasting food from the not-so-heart-healthy menu, and lots of kiosks carrying hand-crafted jewelry.

We would invariably "ooh" and "aah" over industrial looking necklaces and then figure out if we could make something ourselves. One of the headlining bands, I explained, did rocking covers of eighties music like Talking Heads and Huey Lewis.

"Count me in," she said. "Afterwards, we can go to the lesbian karaoke Irish bar? It's close to my place."

I pondered this for a second. I am not a lesbian, and I am actually not a big karaoke fan, but as she described the experience, I couldn't say no.

"It's really great," she went on. "A lot of lesbians come to the place, but gay guys and straights come too. It's also popular with Native Americans. Everyone really feels free to be themselves and everybody really gets along well with each other."

After several hours bouncing between the three stages on Roscoe, four beers, one Italian beef sandwich apiece, and lots of banter about the abundance of high-end strollers, equipped with multiple hide-away cup holders, we headed to the Lincoln Square area.

When we walked into the bar, the owner, a middle-aged woman with jet black hair and the most striking yellow-green eyes I have ever seen, greeted us. It was around 10:30 and still easy to find an open stool. A half hour later, that would no longer be the case.

My friend lugged the bar's bible, the binder with laminated sheets listing all the song titles, to our stools. There must have been hundreds, maybe thousands of titles.

I joked about performing the Elton John classic "Tiny Dancer," intentionally mispronouncing it to "Hold Me Closer, Tony Danza," but I was quickly chickening out of making my karaoke debut. No shortage of other talent, though.

There was a bride-to-be, coyly accessorized in a plastic veil, and her entire posse sitting close to the mic along with a variety of regulars who attended a local music school. Ringers, most of them. I noticed the bar started filling up.

There were ladies on dates with their best lady friend, logo-tee wearing straight guys shooting darts and slamming down shots of tequila, gay men fresh from Halsted Street Market

Days (another street fair that took place that day in Boys Town) . . . and the parade of karaoke stars began.

A bridesmaid (apparently no newcomer to a microphone) started things off with a soulful version of "Killing Me Softly." Then the bride belted out George Michael's "Somebody to Love." Everyone joined in on the chorus as she twirled her veil with her fingers.

A tall twenty-something, baring more than a few piercings, belted out Dolly Parton's "Jolene." Everybody was very tolerant when a young guy felt compelled to go counter-crowd and do Springsteen's "Born in the USA." About an hour into the songfest, someone did an artificially inspirational number from a contemporary musical I wasn't familiar with.

"Damn," the woman next to me pounded her palm on the top of the bar. "They should outlaw this song from karaoke bars everywhere."

In her mid-twenties with cornflower blue eyes, pale skin, and non-descript brown hair styled in a mullet, she went on to explain, "I come from a small town in Ohio. They sang this damn song at our high school's graduation for four straight years."

Those of us within earshot patted her shoulder in consolation. Yes, there ought to be a karaoke law of some sort.

While I did not close the place down, during my night at the lesbian karoke Irish bar, I ended up hearing quite a cavalcade of memory-joggers sung by every kind of person you could imagine. After a day in *Stroller Village*, this was especially heartening.

Seeing that there is a place for EVERYONE, a place of laughter and belonging, is no small thing.

Grateful Dozen Category: Belonging,
August 15, 2010

Remembering Names

"**V**ANESSA'S HAVING HER usual," the Starbucks barista shouted.
I'm not much of a Starbucks patron. For one thing, I don't drink coffee. But this morning, before heading downtown for the day, I didn't have time to make breakfast and I had a Starbucks gift card in my purse.

I had a vision that there was a cinnamon scone with my name on it tilted on display in their glass pastry case. It was drizzled with sweet white icing.

"Vanessa's having her usual."

The barista, a tall, thin man in his early twenties wearing a black logo-decorated baseball cap, repeated the order.

He called down the counter to two other crew members: two women, who were even younger. They were similarly decked out in black slacks and long-sleeved button-down shirts, black baseball caps and green cotton aprons.

The girl closest to the coffee machine, with a fresh-from-the-farm complexion and four piercings in one ear lobe, giggled then pulled out the appropriately-sized cardboard cup.

"This is the second day in a row that you remembered her name now, isn't it?" she teased her co-worker.

"Yes," he replied as she started the process of filling, frothing, and flavoring Vanessa's standing order.

"I have a buffer of about 720 names," he went on. "I am sure the names of most of the people we see all the time are in there. Somewhere."

I confess I was pretty impressed with his recall. When the other girl rang up my order and deducted today's purchase from the balance on my gift card, I didn't even think about how well she retained information.

How did the other barista know what Vanessa's usual was? Did she like her coffee strong or weak? Creamy? Black? Sweet?

Vanessa, a short thirty-something with black and blonde streaked, spiked hair, started fumbling through her handbag looking for her wallet. The big, black leather handbag would barely have qualified as acceptable overhead storage according to any airline's policy.

She seemed happy. She looked up at the three servers and smiled. She must have been happy that the barista remembered her name.

Calling people by their name is an incredibly welcoming gesture, a small way to say, "Yes, *you* matter."

I know that when I make appointments or do other types of professional phone work, I always make a point of repeating the contact's name. Even when I am just leaving a message, after I leave my phone number, I add "John," or "Lorraine," or "Billy Bob," ... "I'm looking forward to talking with you."

Seeing this short scene at the mother-of-all corporate-controlled experience providers was really heartening. And it wasn't even about me. It wasn't even my "usual" that everyone seemed to know.

But it got me thinking that if I did drink coffee, if I did visit a specific café practically every day like Vanessa, I imagined how happy I would be to have my name remembered.

Hearing someone remember your name is no small thing.

Grateful Dozen Category: Belonging, Neighborhood Discoveries,
September, 20, 2010

Ask and It is Given

I HAD MADE AN executive decision. I would go to the bathroom before I took my seat. Why squirm, even for an hour? The crowds would only get worse, I figured, and the next act was not going on for another fifteen minutes.

This was my first trip to the Hyde Park Jazz Festival. It had become a south side tradition for the last four years. Before the neighborhood became a tourist destination for people seeking anything *Obama*, this part of the city was known as an intellectual and cultural Mecca, a very "United Colors of Benetton progressive" sort of neighborhood and home of The University of Chicago.

I was at the assembly hall at the International House, one of many venues the U of C offered for the occasion. The musical menu for the festival featured an abundance of local talent; 150 musicians at fifteen venues over twelve hours.

I knew the pianist who was playing at 3:00 and trusted I would find my way to two or three other sets before heading back home to the other side of town.

It was an old-fashioned, institutional sort of women's lounge. You had to walk down a short flight of marble stairs and turn into a room with about five stalls, including one extra wide one for handicapped access. None of the latches on the stall doors seemed to work very well.

The hot air hand dryer only worked intermittently and there was more pink, goopy soap pooled up on the ancient sink counter than in the dispenser. There was a sign near the mirror announcing something akin to a pledge to keep the premises clean.

Hallelujah, none of the stalls were occupied. I slipped into the middle one, seemingly the cleanest, and began the *hanging ritual*, first draping my purse strap over the hook on the inside of the door, then placing my cotton hoodie over it, hoping that it would hold up for the duration of my visit.

I heard a few other women enter nearby stalls by the time I was pulling down my jeans.

"Excuse me," I heard a meek voice pipe out to the person in the stall next to hers. "There doesn't seem to be any toilet paper here."

For a second, I went into a panic. I had my pants bunched up around my knees and was half sitting and half squatting over an ancient University of Chicago toilet (and I didn't care what their posted pledge about cleanliness said, I was not about to sit squarely on the throne).

Then I found myself moving into an almost Socratic mode of self-inquiry. *Did I forget to check for TP?* Relief spilled over me quickly as I looked to my left. There was TP aplenty behind door number three.

Ah, I thought to myself, as I like to do, time to be grateful. Still in my sitting-squatting pose, I considered my good fortune. I had plenty of toilet paper waiting in readiness by my side.

Even better, I was not at an outdoor venue where I would have had to use a port-a-potty. I may even have had some Kleenex balled up in my purse . . . . Then I heard a different voice.

"Yes, I have some here," the woman from two stalls down called back. "I'll pass it to you under the wall."

Wow. Is this a miracle or something? After the hand-off must have happened, I heard a quiet and grateful thank you. I was still contemplating the simple joy of toilet paper when I walked to the sink to wash my hands. I was struck by another observation.

It was great that there was someone on the other side of the stall wall who was able to provide exactly what was needed. Nine times out of ten, when you ask for something, you can get it.

Remembering to ask is no small thing.

Grateful Dozen Category: Noticing Small Things,
September 28, 2010

My Secret River

I HAVE BEEN LIVING in my apartment on School Street for around eighteen years. It has provided a sense of security, a feeling of familiarity and neighborhood that I really liked.

I developed the habit of walking to my health club when I wanted to sweat, Whole Foods when I wanted to eat something fresh, or Hamlin Park when I longed for the satisfying summer entertainment of watching little leaguers and grown-up boys don their local pizza parlor-sponsored uniforms to play baseball.

I had eased into paying a fairly manageable monthly rent, which I never discounted as a blessing, and, while not best buddies, I always felt I could count on my upstairs neighbors in an emergency.

But over the past six months to a year, I was getting the feeling that my karma here was over.

My landlady became vocal in objecting to certain visitors I had over; work to repair my upstairs neighbor's pipes, requiring tearing apart my ceiling in a few places, was scheduled without advance notice. When I tried to rent half of the unused garage behind the three-flat to store my new car, I was turned down with no explanation.

I had been planning on moving for a while, ideally to a building where I could purchase and make a permanent home, but I was hoping this move would be on my timetable.

Yet, here I was heading into winter with a very concrete goal of finding a new place to live within a couple weeks; one that was in a safe neighborhood and close to public transportation, a place that was roomy enough to set up a desk for what had become a predominantly work-at-home lifestyle, and a place where I could pay about the same rent as I had been paying for my deal on School Street.

Oh yes, and it had to have a garage—a covered, off-street parking place for Freyla, the name I had given my new VW Jetta.

I poured over Craigslist posts and contacted numerous property management companies, not to mention Apartment Hunters, Apartment People, and just about every apartment locating outfit I could find.

The short timetable made the search discouraging. There are simply not as many rental properties in Chicago with December 1st leases as there are with May 1st or October 1st leases.

I was anticipating having to settle in some fundamental way after setting an intention where settling was no longer an option. Too often, though, apartments with garage spaces were in elevator buildings and were tiny and without character.

Just over a week ago, after visiting a variety of elevator buildings with shoebox-sized apartments with $150 a month garage rent, I found a Craigslist post for a large, sunny apartment in a two-flat with hardwood floors and a two-car garage behind the building.

They wanted to rent it for November 1st and had obviously gone past the date. It was in a neighborhood I was not very familiar with: a few blocks of two-flats and Chicago style brick bungalows flanked by 100 year-old elms, only steps away from the exclusive Ravenswood Manor area.

After pacing the length of the unit several times, looking for flaws and finding few things I could complain about, I started imagining filling the second bedroom with my office essentials and the pantry with my beloved red Rival crock pot and Jack LaLanne power juicer.

I asked for a lease application and took a walk around what I hoped would become my new neighborhood.

I had forgotten that the north branch of the Chicago River runs just a few blocks east of Mozart Street. There's a narrow strip of houses in Chicago that are situated with their yards right up against the river. Many of these houses have small boats tied up to little wooden piers only steps from their back doors. Others have incredible gardens, nestled away undisturbed by virtue of their location.

I walked to Wilson Avenue, which connects Ravenswood Manor to the more active area of Lincoln Square. I stood on the bridge there for a while meditating on the tree branches, recently freed of their golden leaves by early November winds.

I looked in both directions, at the boats in the water, at the changing width of the river, at the trees and yards and houses that ran along its banks, at other bridges I could see in the distance.

I relished the scene's sort of moodiness—and my own sense of surprise. I found a new place to live at a very challenging time of year, in a location that feels like being out in the country but is only one block from the Montrose bus; only a few blocks from the river.

I felt lucky, but I also wanted to acknowledge myself for taking up a challenge life presented me.

If I didn't feel I had to move now, I wouldn't have gone looking for a new home and neighborhood. If I wasn't willing to risk the security I knew, I would not have discovered this hidden corner of nature in the city, this place where change and constancy seemed to get along so well.

Discovering your secret river is no small thing.

Grateful Dozen Category: Neighborhood Discoveries,
November 11, 2011

Making Friends—
One Stranger at a Time

I PULLED UP TO the Enterprise Rent-A-Car on Western near
Grace on Tuesday morning at around 7:15.
    My contract said that I needed to get the car back by 7:30.
Not wanting to run the risk of paying for more than the two
days I had budgeted for driving my niece up to music camp in

Egg Harbor, I made sure I got my orange red little Kia refueled and parked back on the lot before the office opened.

A slightly-built Hispanic man with a receding hairline, was standing only inches in front of the glass door. He was reading and re-reading the information about hours.

"I see someone in the office, but no one has unlocked the door yet," he reported as I walked towards the spot where he had positioned himself, no doubt to be first in line.

"They should be open soon," he added, sounding more intent on reassuring himself than anything else.

I don't know why, but the actual thoughts that were running through my head just poured out. We were sort of in the same situation.

"I just came back from Door County," I announced. "I was driving my niece up to music camp. She plays the violin. I have a car, a Honda Civic, but it's over fifteen years old, and I wanted her to be comfortable. It's almost a five hour drive," I said before getting to the biggest concern on my mind. "I wanted to make sure I got the car back early so they wouldn't charge extra."

The man smiled. He understood.

"All my children came to Chicago this weekend for Father's Day. Two from San Juan, one from Virginia, and Estefania came in from L.A. They made me rent a van so we could go everywhere together."

"They bought me a Kindle," he added with an unabashed outpouring of enthusiasm then sighed. "It was the best Father's Day I ever had."

While we waited for the office to open, he told me about the first few books he downloaded with his new Kindle, about how much he loves to read, especially since his retirement only six months earlier.

He gushed about how much he loved his family. I found out that he was in a hurry to get through processing his rental return. He had to get home and drive his eldest son, Braulio, to the airport for a 9:30 flight. "Don't worry," I told him, "Where do you live? Humboldt Park? That's not that far. I'll drive you."

When the office opened and he handed in his car key, he asked if someone from the agency could drive him home. Since they only offered transportation to an L station or bus stop, he decided to take me up on my offer.

We both knew driving to O'Hare on the Kennedy during rush hour was a crapshoot, and the faster we could get him home, the better his chances would be to help his son make his flight.

We continued our conversation in my car. We talked about the current debate about making Puerto Rico a state. "What's up with that?" I asked. "What do the people in your neighborhood think?"

I told him about my trip to Door County with my fifteen year-old niece.

I had been looking forward to having some bonding time with her, but she was exhausted from worrying about the competition at Birch Creek and slept practically the whole time we were together. "She knows you were there for her," my passenger reminded me.

I decided I could tell him about my other activity in Door County, visiting my friend Chris who was in hospice at a nursing home in Sturgeon Bay.

I had spent most of the previous day with him, developing my skills at packing his wheelchair into the tiny Kia trunk and going on small excursions—a local diner for lunch and to a sporting goods store where we got him a baseball cap so he could cheer on his beloved Brewers in style.

"He has cancer?" my new friend asked. "My son-in-law had cancer. I was with my daughter when he passed. It happened so quickly from when he was told he was sick. He was the best man you would ever want to know," his voice wavered, recollections refreshed.

"... A pastor. Only fifty-two. The church arranged for grief counseling for the whole family. That was very good, I think," he nodded, noticing that we were approaching the great metal sculpture of the Puerto Rican flag that appears to undulate across Division Street. He pointed out his house.

He asked if he could pay me something for driving him home. It wasn't necessary, I told him. Moments after he swung the door open, before he stepped out, he turned towards me and extended his hand.

"What's your name?" he asked.

"Deborah. What's yours?"

"Hector," he said and smiled, adding his thanks.

In the ten minutes it took to get from the rent-a-car office on Western to Hector's house, a relatively short distance, it seemed like we covered a lot of territory. We talked about love and family, politics and grief. We became fully fleshed out human beings to each other. And to think, it all started at Enterprise, waiting for the office to open.

Making friends, one stranger at a time, should be a primary enterprise of everyone. When you can sense the personhood of someone, even someone who you will never see again—it's no small thing.

Grateful Dozen Category: Belonging,
June 24, 2011

Resolution

MY MOTHER DIED last Friday. Several people have since expressed shock about her passing. I think, though, she had been in the process of dying for a while. And now I am in the process of trying to understand my feelings about our relationship and her passing.

I know my experience of my mother was different from how my older sisters experienced her, different than how her friends experienced her, and different from the way the ladies she entertained with her singing at *Tease*, the beauty parlor she frequented, experienced her.

About three years ago she began having falls. The first happened while walking from the driveway to my sister's front door for Thanksgiving dinner. We bandaged and wrapped my mother's head until appetizers and main courses were served as she didn't want to miss them.

The second occurred in the Oak Park Temple parking lot before a Friday night Sabbath service. The third occurred as she walked from her parked car on her way to Tease for her weekly hair appointment.

She tore some ligaments in her hand during that fall, necessitating hand surgery and physical therapy, giving my sister and I a good excuse to retire her car keys and sell her low-mileage tank, i.e., her beloved beige Buick.

After that point, I started making regular Sunday visits to spend a little time with her and take her to the grocery store. Her hips were starting to hurt. With her mobility weakening, she could barely walk without a cane or walker, but she loved to push the shopping cart up and down the aisles of the Jewel.

She leaned on the cart and didn't have to put much weight on her legs. After several months of shopping this way, I decided to change our routine. It was a very time-consuming way to shop.

I started to take her to the store, sit her on the bench near the registers, pick up all the items on her list then call her to the check-out specifically to sign the credit card receipt.

Around October, she didn't feel like walking any more, and I started to take her credit card and bank card and do her shopping and banking for her, signing her name when required.

My sister and I started exploring the possibilities of hip replacement surgery in the fall. Her right hip seemed to be the biggest source of pain for her. She stopped walking altogether mid-December. While she was waiting—and waiting and waiting—to have her "surgery" (she was scheduled and canceled three times) we hired home-care workers to stay with her 24/7.

While we re-directed our energies into discovering and, ideally, medically correcting whatever was standing in the way of replacing her worn-out joint, we learned that our mother had bone metastases, lesions of cancer, from some unknown source. My mother, sister, and I then began a different journey.

Barbara, who was not very involved in my mother's life prior to fall of last year, became chief internet researcher, physician interrogator, and coordinator of homecare staff. I kept up with my visits and shopping duties, although now I was also trying to keep mom's house in Doritos and Coke for her contracted posse whose main job was carrying her to the commode.

Both my sister and I talked to the physical therapists and homecare staff that visited our mother and compared notes. My sister and I began talking more often, and about topics more meaningful than we ever had before.

Four weeks ago, we got her new oncologist to admit her to Rush University Medical Center so that we could have other tests done as an inpatient.

They performed the hip surgery we had tried for so long to see her through—only now the medical experts did it so that her right leg bone would literally not break. My sister and I placed her at a skilled nursing facility for required rehab.

I took her back to Rush for a day of outpatient follow-up visits just over a week ago. The next day, after observing shaking and vomiting, the nursing facility sent her back to the medical center by ambulance.

I met her at the ER. She was x-rayed and hydrated, put on oxygen and asked if she knew where she was by a flurry of good-looking young residents. Eventually, she was admitted.

Over the next few days, as I realized that her "confusion" was more than confusion (each day, she lost more of her ability to communicate), specialists conferred with me on all range of treatment options, none of which came with a guaranteed result or benefit.

My sister, our family's chief medical officer, was on a cruise ship in the Grenadines. I was on my own, wanting to do the right thing.

Two days after being admitted, when it was clear that she was going through multi-organ shut-down, I placed her on hospice. The next day, when my sister and brother-in-law got back to town, they pretty much headed directly to the hospital.

Once on hospice, where she was given a potent IV cocktail for relaxation, her involuntary jerking movements stopped. That made me feel it was okay to invite her fourteen-year-old granddaughter to see her.

The four of us spent last Friday afternoon and evening with her. I swabbed her dry lips with a sponge-tipped, water-soaked stick. There wasn't much more I could do.

We left my mother's room at 8:00 and caught a light bite near the medical center. Not two hours after I got home, her floor nurse called me to say that she had passed away.

I have an odd appreciation for how things actually worked out. What most people want, I think, are "happy endings." The best we can hope for and what we can receive by embracing life as it is, are perfect resolutions. And aren't all resolutions *perfect*?

In her dying from kidney failure instead of experiencing the advancement of her bone cancer, my mother found an exit strategy that was probably kinder.

My sister, who had been pulling extra duty in service to my mother, my youngest niece, and her husband badly needed a vacation. She completed hers as planned. And I needed to feel like an *adult*.

Marveling at the process of life, including death, is no small thing.

Grateful Dozen category: Belonging,
April 14, 2011

Canción Familiar

HERE I WAS in Madrid on the first days of my long-anticipated European adventure with John. In the preceding weeks, we had spent hours together online scouring the Agoda website and TripAdvisor picking out hotels and reading Rick Steves' recommendations on what to do if you only had two days to spend in Seville.

We managed to get to our hotel from the Madrid airport using the Metro (which would have been a snap if we weren't lugging over-packed suitcases through their multi-level, elevator-challenged stations).

John already had a few friendly conversations with a couple bartenders (en Espanol) as we educated ourselves on tapas, and I felt like sighing, "Eh, Toto. I don't think we're in Kansas anymore."

My first observations were about the little ways the locals (dare I call them Madridniks?) did things differently. They didn't seem to eat dinner before 9:00. They also, I soon learned, might not come home from a night of drinking until 6:00 in the morning.

When we got to our hotel room, we couldn't figure out how to turn on the lights in the room. It turned out that you had to put the key card in the wall. Being very energy conscious, they designed hotel rooms so that guests could not leave lights on when they went out.

We also couldn't help but notice how crowded the streets became at night. Couples or girlfriends linked arm in arm Euro-style or families with young children in tow filled Plaza Mayor or the Gran Via eating, drinking, and shopping (how the Spaniards love to shop!) late into the evening.

Wow, what an introduction to Spain! Our hotel was only a few hundred feet up a little alley from the Gran Via (their 5th Avenue).

Tiny bodegas, where we could buy juice or coffee, were tucked away in alleys close to trendy night clubs and upscale stores and eateries. Everything was very foreign, but also very Yankee friendly.

I was loving our walks—and walking, eating and drinking was basically what we did during the first stop in our eighteen-day plan. We looked at the architecture and monuments (every square seemed to have a very, very old church and a statue with some guy on a horse).

We ogled at typical street scenes like the six-block long line we saw near the Museo de Jamon (Ham Museum) a local deli that featured the country's best Serrano and Iberico hams. Hundreds of people were queued up to buy Christmas lottery tickets.

We took frequent rests from our walks, sitting at local tabernas, drinking tinto or rioja and trying to estimate how much the same glass of wine and small appetizer plate would cost in the U.S. We seemed able to leave our short, and frequent, wine and tapas stops, happily fed and quenched for ten or fifteen Euros.

I loved the new sights and smells that surrounded me. I loved having a partner (an excellent map-reader) to share the adventure with, but I realized in some ways I felt isolated.

I thrive on words. I revel in small talk with strangers. I like hearing people's everyday stories, and I don't speak Spanish. Not beyond the rudimentary phrases, "Hola," or "Buenas noches," "Gracias," and "cerveza fria por favour."

So often, I would overhear conversations on the street and would tug at John's jacket. "What did they say?" I'd ask him.

Fortunately, we were never far from music. The sounds of gypsy accordion melodies or crowd-pleasing Spanish guitar classics filled the squares.

Street musicians could be found almost everywhere people would gather. They'd position coffee cans or their instrument cases nearby to encourage donations. Being able to recognize a song allowed me to feel at home in a place where I did not speak the native tongue.

Monday night, we made our way towards Pura Cepa, a wonderful restaurant a friend recommended. With a Metro map in hand, we transferred from the five line to the six line, took the escalator up a few flights then walked up the very long ramp of the O'Donnell stop up to street level.

The pedestrian tunnel was washed in a bluish light. I could see the thin silhouette of a single guitarist, case open at his feet, twenty yards ahead; the only other person in the tunnel. The notes that came out of his guitar were simple and clear.

"Isn't this an old Beatles' song?" I asked John as we reached the steps to the street. He squeezed my hand and sang along with the street musician, a tune I learned later was one of his Fab Four favorites.

". . . This boy would be good for you. . . ." Here I was in Madrid, welcoming new experiences and feeling very much at home.

Being touched by a familiar song is no small thing.

Grateful Dozen Category: Tourist Eyes,
December 31, 2011

Midnight in Paris

JOHN AND I have been back from our European adventure for four days now. On our first night back, we devoured a dinner of steak and fresh broccoli—red meat and green vegetables seeming to be one of the few food cravings we could not satisfy in Spain or France.

We got our bodies re-acclimated to operating on the correct time zone (i.e. we were falling asleep at night and actually waking up in the morning) and we paid those bills that we knew would come due within days of our return (thanks to Outlook alarms).

We also made time to sort through our snapshots and post them on online galleries in order to share them with our friends. This was a magical process in itself.

I remember when I was a kid, how after a vacation we would drop off rolls of film from our Instamatic at our local Walgreen's where they would send them out to a processor for development.

It would take about a week before we could actually see any glossies. Perhaps weeks later, we would invite relatives or friends over for dinner and to see our vacation book; a padded vinyl-covered album that contained our photos. Because of development costs, we didn't take more photos than what we thought would turn out. We pretty much put every image we took in "the book."

John and I probably took hundreds of photos in our eighteen days abroad and yet, it didn't feel like our intention to build an image library for memories interfered with our being present to what we were experiencing in any moment.

We had fun when we would retreat to our hotel for the evening and download images from the last day or two onto his laptop. We deleted a few pics during these reviews but saved the task of serious editing for our return. Yesterday, we posted separate collections from each place we visited to run as slide shows on Kodak's site.

There were three stages to this activity. Each, involving the mind and heart, contained their own special pleasures.

First, we went through a selection process. Fortunately, John and I agreed on most choices. We wanted to have some tourist shots, some record of our visits to important attractions, but we mostly took street shots. When compiling our collection, we looked for shots that captured what we were feeling where the shot was taken, or we looked for something that conveyed a sense of uniqueness about a place.

We chose keeping pictures of unexpected finds, like a UPS truck in Barcelona's Ciutat Vella (Old City), and artfully composed shots, like one of our reflections in a bookstore window on Paris' left bank.

We wanted to avoid just putting out everything we took. We wanted to choose the best five, not twenty-five, pictures of the hanging hams in Spain's delicatessens and tapas bars, and the most Parisian-looking images of sidewalk café chairs arranged for people-watching.

Then we went on to the task of captioning and, like cartoonists for the New Yorker, had fun trying to compose wry observations for some of our pictures.

We included small notes on locations so that we could remember where we saw something, but most of our verbiage reflected our personal sense of humor. For a photo of two waiters smoking on break just outside an upscale Paris café, we added the comment, "At these prices, they should be working." For a picture of me in a garden copying the pose of a nearby sculpture of a nude woman, hands clasped seductively behind her head, back arched, we wrote, "Statue imitating Deb."

The last stage of creating our online image albums was re-living. We must have viewed each shot several times, individually and then as part of a slideshow, before we decided to share the Kodak link with our friends.

Each image seemed to tap into a well of experiences. When we remembered each place, we remembered how we felt at the time. We recalled whether we arrived somewhere on foot or by Metro, if we were hungry or whether we snagged a croissant or crepe on the way, if we got lost that morning or if we felt in flow, if we thought something was funny, how the air smelled, and sometimes we actually seemed to hear whatever music might have been playing when we were in a scene.

We delighted in each private slideshow. After all, although we wanted to share our pictures, the process of creating roadmaps to our best memories, we understood, was really for us.

Using images to trigger a felt experience and actually relive that moment is no small thing.

Grateful Dozen Category: Tourist Eyes, Belonging,
January 17, 2012

The Reading Room

WHEN I WAS growing up, I remember the two upstairs bathrooms of our house as reading rooms.

In the turquoise bathroom off my parents' master bedroom, Herman Wouk's *Winds of War* seemed to have taken up permanent residence. My mother was a dedicated reader although obviously not a graduate of any Evelyn Wood Speed Reading course.

Weeks may have gone by before page markings showed any progress. With husband and daughters asleep, during late night hours, my mother used to like to smoke a cigarette on the toilet and read.

My sister Ronna's favorite book, even in paperback, seemed too big to pick up and finish under any circumstances let alone in short bathroom sessions, yet I always spied it in the pink bathroom that we shared with our sister Barbara.

At fourteen, I wondered how she could digest such a tome, yet I could count on her book being somewhere on the dull pink patterned vanity. She never got tired of reading and re-reading the classic. I never seemed to get beyond the first page.

"... Scarlett O'Hara was not beautiful, but men seldom realized it when caught by her charm as the Tarleton twins were."

I hadn't thought about reading on the toilet for years, not until recently. John seems to have a library of magazines in his bathroom, and yes, I have rekindled my appreciation for the indulgence.

His bathroom library includes local magazines with restaurant reviews and a season's worth of *New Yorkers*; maybe an issue or two of *Esquire* or *The Atlantic*.

The New Yorker is always good for a cartoon if not for some kind of article on something I would never have thought about but will undoubtedly bring into conversations now that a subject's been called to my attention. (Just the other week, I read about the popularity of workplace novels in China. Have you ever heard of the genre?)

Reading for pleasure or to stay culturally informed, reading without the goal of subject mastery, seems to be hard to make time for.

Yes, people will crowd subway cars with their Kindles to kill time, reading page turners by virtually turning the pages. I will pick up junk magazines at the health club so I can pour over topics like "Which celeb looks best in the Michael Kors frock?" while I raise my heart rate and marvel at how much I can sweat.

But this kind of reading does not impart the same pleasure. It's done to fill time. And reading to fill time between doing other things does not seem to confer the same level of reflection, sense of discovery or respect for language. Besides, some kinds of reading are done in public. And bathroom reading . . . it's oh so private.

Isn't it a special joy to retreat to a clean and quiet chamber and, accompanied by the barely audible buzz of the fluorescent tube, scan an issue of *Rolling Stone* and learn about some unsung hero, a Pentagon whistleblower, or contemplate the next restaurant you want to try after you have replenished your bank account a little?

Bathroom reading is about private time, a luxury for sure. It's also about openness and curiosity—and about paper.

Yes, I suppose you could consider me a Tory in the Cyber Revolution, but I love seeing words on paper, and I love the eclectic range and serendipity of what reading material you might find in someone else's bathroom, their reading room.

Maybe the bathroom is the last place someone would bring their laptop; the last android free zone. Maybe bathroom reading rooms represent the last place where we read what is in front of us, surrendering and respecting chance, and not pre-select material as the result of a Google search.

Having a private relationship with words and taking little reflective retreats—even in five minute doses—is no small thing.

Grateful Dozen Category: Musings—Adventures With
My Mind, February 3, 2012

Other People's Lessons

I HAVE BEEN THINKING about *lessons* a lot lately. No more so than today. My older sister has been sick, and I have taken on the weekly task of driving our niece Emma to her violin lesson.

When I have listened to Emma at her lessons these past few weeks, I have been in awe. Yes, she sounds nothing like the four-year-old girl who first picked up a quarter-sized violin twelve years ago and, thanks to Mr. Suzuki, learned how to bow with coarse strokes and the aid of memorized nursery rhymes.

Not only do the sounds that come out of her violin these days sound like music, it is obvious that the music is deeply felt. The music she makes is sublime.

The other week, Emma confessed to me, "I don't always like to practice. But I love my lessons."

All I can think of, as a way to explain this passion, is that during her lessons Emma's teacher engages her in ways that help her develop her awareness.

Her teacher, Holly, will ask her questions like: *How does that sound to you? What do you think the fingering for that arpeggio should be? Do you think you're putting too much pressure on the strings? What do you think you need to practice on this week?*

Mixed in with tips for improvement, she'll make comments like, *That sounds much better than it did two weeks ago,* or *I can tell you've been practicing that.*

When trying to respond to such thoughtful questions, Emma seems to search for the right words to describe the subtle qualities she's noticed in her own playing.

She'll say things like "It feels awkward when I do it that way," or "I can get it right when I go slow, but not when I bring it up tempo." In an ongoing discussion with her teacher, or with herself, she hits on adjustments to try.

In observing Emma's Wednesday afternoon one-on-one today, I saw the lesson in *all* lessons: to look at the result you just got and ask, "What do I want to do more of or less of next time? How can I make this better? How can I make my experience easier? How can I acknowledge my mastery in this instance and chart out a new learning objective?"

For Emma, this might be about moving from Schubert to Mendelssohn to Bruck.

I loved sitting in on Emma's violin lesson today. It felt good to think of progress, in any pursuit, as the natural outcome of practice with conscious awareness and support.

Remembering that **anybody's lesson** is **everybody's lesson** is no small thing.

Grateful Dozen Category: Belonging,
April 11, 2012

In Good Company

WHEN I WAS seven or eight, family road trips to the Wisconsin Dells or to South Haven, Michigan usually included different sorts of games to pass the time.

I would bend one arm like the woman in the *We Can Do It* World War II propaganda poster, then pump my fist up and down until passing truck drivers, who were on to the game, would honk their horns.

My mother would lead me and my sister in rounds of *Twenty Questions* and I would go beyond animal, vegetable, or mineral start-up strategies to pull out telling clues. These pastimes were reserved for relatively short trips.

For me and John's road trip to New Orleans, occupying ourselves for many, MANY hours was a much bigger issue. We left for Memphis on Christmas morning (basically an eight hour trip without stops), then continued to New Orleans the next day, driving another six hours.

Coming back, we drove ten hours from the Crescent City to St. Louis, stopping only for gas, coffee, and clean restrooms, then drove for five more hours before we could pull into our garage.

Before we left, we thought a good book on tape (CD actually) was in order. In a recent *Sunday Times* book section, we found some recommendations under the guise of Christmas gift ideas.

The *Times* reviewer practically gushed about the audiobook edition of Junot Diaz's most recent release, *This is How You Lose Her*. Read by the author, the tales of a young Dominican man growing up in Jersey seemed to have compelling biographical elements making it hard not to wonder where the lines between fiction and real life may have blurred.

I fell in love with one of his earlier books, *The Brief Wondrous Life of Oscar Wao*, so Amazon made an easy sale. I checked out the opening lines and posted reviews before I confirmed credit card information.

"I'M NOT A BAD GUY. I know how that sounds—defensive, unscrupulous—but it's true. I'm like everybody else: weak, full of mistakes, but basically good."

I could tell quickly that there was a character here, a real person coming to me as a fictional hero. I suspected that after a few hours bearing witness to his confidence, I would love his candor and question his judgment.

This turned out to be more than true. The language of Yunior's narrative rang true.

We wanted to really understand his experience. What would it be like to be an immigrant child growing up in New Jersey? To live close to a part of the Atlantic Ocean that you never got to see, let alone swim in? To witness your father exercise his best networking skills just to find a barber that could cut your *pelo malo*, your "bad" (kinky) hair?

The book came in five CDs. We divided our in-car listening time between Diaz's alter ego, radio stations that weren't churchy talk shows, and a handful of CDs we brought (Louie Armstrong and Pine Leaf Boys) to psyche us up for our Louisiana holiday. We wanted to savor the stories, the role of confidante, moments of recognition.

We laughed out loud at the way he described his mother and her prayer group friends (The Four Horsefaces of the Apocalypse) and discussed the chronology of the stories to make sure we understood the real life sequence of events.

We asked ourselves, "Didn't he mention that his brother Rafa died of cancer in disc one, but didn't talk about his last job at The Yarn Barn until much later?"

We wanted the stories to go on, and on, even after the narrator brought us back to the beginning, thematically, with a chapter entitled "The Cheater's Guide to Love."

In all of Yunior's reflections, perhaps we heard the disparate voices of our own optimism and cynicism, telling us that if we knew better we can do better, but somehow not quite believing our ability to change in fundamental ways.

Yes, we loved hearing the street musicians outside the Café du Monde, reveled in the great dinner we had at Herbsaint, and puffed up with pride at the discovery of an actual farmer's market in the warehouse district, but spending hours in the car with Junot Diaz was another highlight of the trip.

Sinking into universal truths through the telling of another's *personal* experience is a special gift.

Having the good company of a great storyteller is no small thing.

Grateful Dozen Category: Belonging, January 8, 2013

I Got the Last One

I DON'T EAT A lot of sweets or junk food. Really. I try to eat healthy. I love fresh vegetables (except Brussels sprouts).

I'll generally buy hormone-free meats and when I check a carton of eggs before they end up in my shopping cart, I look for large (but not *jumbo*) Omega-3, brown eggs laid by happy chickens who reside in the same time zone.

I keep a small container of shelled walnuts in my cupboard for when I feel the urge to snack, but, I confess, sometimes I just want something . . . something sweet. Hell, I want something chocolate, and there's no substitute.

The other day, I was fighting such a craving.

My first strategy was to find some nuts. After getting past the child-proof capped clear plastic container—why does opening food packaging have to be so hard?—I nibbled some walnuts. This did not satisfy me.

Then I scoured my cupboards and storage bins for trail mix or the kind of semi-sweet biscuits I might serve with a St. Andre or triple cream cheese, but I couldn't rustle up any type of sweet cracker either.

I thought about making toast and sampling some homemade jams a few of my friends gifted me out of their passion for canning, but I didn't even get around to plugging in the toaster. Really, I wanted chocolate. Plum ambrosia was just not going to cut it.

I was almost ready to go to the closest Starbucks for a cakey chocolate breakfast muffin when I remembered John came home from work a few days earlier with half a box of Two-Bite® brownies from Trader Joe's. There must have been some sort of celebration where he worked and he came home with a modest care package of remnants.

Sure enough, I found the clear, half-a-hatbox sized container on the small granite-topped table near the refrigerator. There was one little brownie left along with a few brown crumbs dusting the bottom of the package. They'd been in my house a few days now. I studied the expiration date and list of ingredients on the oversized label.

A moment of guilt passed through me as I separated the lid from the bottom of the container and tested the two-bite brownie for edibility. I squeezed it between my thumb and forefinger and still found a little springiness.

Two bites later, I rinsed out the container and threw the evidence in the recycling bin.

My chocolate craving was satisfied, and I felt positively gleeful. I couldn't believe I was so happy about eating a slightly stale thimbleful of sugar and cocoa.

Ha, *I got the last one*. That was it. I was so happy I almost danced around my kitchen.

In my early twenties, I remember fuming quietly to myself when my roommate or her boyfriend consumed the last beer in the fridge. I was too much of a pleaser back then to tell them that if I bought beer, I expected one to be around when I wanted it.

I never argued when I saw a promissory note from them announcing that our beer supply would be restocked after their next grocery trip, but I just let my disappointment fester inside.

*Sometimes you just want something **when** you want it.* Maybe you want a special kind of tool in the middle of a project or a crisp twenty when an unanticipated social plan comes together quickly.

Getting something you want *when* you want it is a small glimpse of heaven for me; an actual situation when you can see your needs fulfilled without having to do something first. It feels like a sign that what you want is already available.

Consuming the last of *anything* is special. It makes me feel chosen. Lucky. Blessed.

Taking the last bite of a two-bite brownie is no small thing.

Grateful Dozen Category: Feeling Like A Winner,
Noticing Small Things, October 21, 2013

Tearing Up

S OMETIMES I HAVE tried to stop them from flowing. I
think this reaction is more about not wanting to make
a companion uncomfortable or about feeling judged as
being weak.

I know I'm not alone. Except for showing grief at a funeral,
strong displays of emotion are generally frowned upon. Boys
aren't supposed to cry, and women who cry—they're labeled as
too sensitive.

When tears have formed in my eyes and rolled down my
cheeks, my first reaction is often betrayal. I'll get upset that my
emotions can so easily trump my will when it comes to how I
want to show myself to the world.

Then there are times when I feel betrayed by an opposite
phenomenon, when I want to relieve myself of frustrations

or resentments, and I somehow can't bring myself to cry. I know I'd find some respite in letting things out this way, but sometimes it seems I've already shut the door.

As a feeling and expressive person, I think I've taken comfort from Dickens' words.

"Heaven knows we need never be ashamed of our tears, for they are rain upon the blinding dust of earth, overlying our hard hearts. I was better after I had cried, than before—more sorry, more aware of my own ingratitude, more gentle."

This past week, I have been grappling with the subject of tears in a different way. The inner debate over whether they should be restrained or encouraged was not my struggle. The hurts tears could potentially have helped heal were not mine.

One good friend invited me to lunch the other day and shared a personal story, now over a month past being news, about being involved in a car accident as a pedestrian. She had barely talked to anyone but closest family following the incident and has been giving her full attention to physical therapy, sleeping, and respecting her inclination for solitude.

She shared that she couldn't even remember details of the accident other than to say she was glad to be alive and felt grateful that neither the driver of the car nor the witness abandoned her while she waited for the ambulance.

She relayed how just talking about the accident made her cry and she didn't know why. She didn't want to cry. She told me she couldn't remember much and took her inability to recall the details as a signal to back off, as an alarm that she was not ready to unravel some things yet.

I talked to another friend earlier this week that was in the middle of a depression. She confessed that she felt like crying *all the time.* She had undergone quadruple bypass surgery just weeks ago and still had a lot to process.

She has been dealing with physical discomfort, frustration over how her medical team handled her, financial stresses, and not having family around to help her manage daily activities.

Wow, I couldn't do anything in either case to make my friends feel better except to respect their individual relationship with crying.

I noticed my impulse to want to encourage my friend who was in the car accident to cry and then to follow her tears to the source of what she's holding in, but I realized she already felt too vulnerable to take this trip. Not now. I listened to my other friend, in starts and stops, as she expressed her fears and worries between sobs.

One wanted to be alone until she regained her strength and confidence. The other friend, I think, was overwhelmed by how alone she felt when being *alone* was the last thing she wanted. She may have been comforted, to some extent, by me simply witnessing her tears.

My respect for tears has only grown. People may let them flow or may hold them back. Although tears have been referred to as "God's way of cleansing the heart," I can see their power in a more direct way.

Robert Herrick, a 17th century English cleric said, *"Tears are the noble language of eyes, and when true love of words is destitute, the eye, by tears, speak while the tongue is mute."*

Tears are a language that can express things words cannot approximate. Letting them flow or not is like making a declaration or deciding to rely on the eloquence of silence.

That tears can speak in such a way is no small thing.

Grateful Dozen Category: Noticing Small Things, Musings—
Adventures with My Mind, January 27, 2014

Dear Deer

IT SEEMS SIMPLE enough; locating a recycling center. But I haven't actually found it to be so. My building doesn't have a special receptacle for recyclables, but I like to avoid taking up extra space in landfills.

So, I'll collect glass bottles, plastic containers, cans, and newspapers in a little blue plastic garbage can and drive full bins to a set of labeled dumpsters at a neighborhood recycling center.

I thought there was one at Horner Park and drove a full can there only to be informed by the security guard that they had to remove the dumpster because people were using it to dump all sorts of *garbage*. Imagine that.

I consulted online postings about the city's recycling program but didn't know if the locations listed were current. The 17th District police station, which used to be a recycling site, suggested I go to the parking lot at Northeastern College. They were supposed to have a big recycling center there.

I hadn't been there for years. Northeastern is a small, teaching school just past the Montrose Cemetery and Crematorium, by a strip of small factories. Along with academic and recreation buildings, the sixty-seven-acre campus contains a small nature preserve. I used to take walks through the trails there with a friend.

Sure enough, after turning off of Pulaski and following the signs pointing to the recycling center, I found myself in a smallish parking lot on the edge of a wooded area with a family of deer watching me.

I was just shy of fuming over the great lengths I had to go through to dispose of my plastic water bottles responsibly when I tripped on a sight that melted my heart.

While the deer didn't hang out by the dumpsters, they weren't afraid of grazing near the pavement either. They obviously didn't like people to come too close, but they liked a lot of the things visitors left behind like discarded remnants of sandwiches.

I observed one deer nuzzling a white candy bar wrapper, pushing it with her snout until she decided it contained nothing for her.

It's so great to find nature in unexpected places; to see fresh flowers in a modest corner cafe or trees in the lobby of an office building.

It's also a treat to see anything or anyone act *naturally*. Not being self-conscious is part of this equation. The family of deer didn't seem to be ruffled by my presence. They tolerated me walking close, but not too close, while I snapped a series of photographs. When they had enough, they simply ran away.

Don't most of us get a charge out of seeing a child or animal doing just about anything because *how* they do things is a natural expression of who they are?

The deer family had friends in the woods. I watched six in total run behind the trees and out of sight before dragging my little blue bin out from the back seat of my car.

I realized I must have been watching them for about ten minutes. During this time, my mission of sorting cans and bottles and paper products was suspended.

Putting agendas on hold in order to revel in an unexpected encounter with nature is no small thing.

Grateful Dozen Category: Beauty, Surprise,
August 8, 2014

Looking for Signs

A WEEK BEFORE THE ball drop in Times Square and other traditions observed to welcome the new year, I talked to my friend Joanne on the phone.

"This is going to be your year," she told me with conviction.

She listened without judgment so many times this past year, times when my heart was heavy or when I felt very unsure of myself. The actual phrase she used sounded like the *Year of the Rooster* or the *Year of the Rat* in Chinese Zodiac parlance.

She told me 2015 was going to be the **Year of Deb**.

Inspired by her pronouncement, I made a **Year of Deb** poster for my office which I hung just to the right of my desk. It showcased a favorite piece of art and my intention to have a very satisfying and fulfilling year.

I assumed that surrounding myself with encouragement was my responsibility, but I noticed myself looking for signs from the universe that supported this notion.

Last week, when I was driving home from errands, I turned at the corner of Wilson and Sacramento, as I do basically every time I come home. I wasn't sure I was seeing correctly, but I could have sworn two small yard signs bearing my name, were planted in the corner lot.

Is this for real? I wondered. I pass this spot almost every day, and I generally introduce myself by this shortened version of *Deborah*. Seeing this D**eb** sign, like Joanne's prediction, made me feel that 2015 is going to be my year.

A day after I first glimpsed the sign, despite a nasty wind chill, I trudged out with my camera to inspect it. Yes, indeed, the sign bore my name. It was simply a campaign tool for local candidate, but I chose to attach extra significance to seeing my name on a neighbor's lawn.

A couple days later, a friend emailed to tease me about my name being on signs all over town.

Well, my name is not exactly plastered all over town, but I expect I'd find quite a few D**eb** signs within the 33rd ward. When I studied the sign after my initial drive-by, I saw that the last name **Mell** was displayed in small print on the bottom and that the placard was decorated with light blue stripes and a spattering of red stars, the style of the city's official flag.

Of course, I thought, Deb Mell is seeking re-election as alderman of my ward. The signs will probably be up through February 24th when the elections will be held.

For the last several days, I've noticed getting excited every time I drive past MY sign. I know I'm not the **Deb** referred to in the sign, but I'd like to think that the sign is *for me.*

People do this all the time. We can *choose* to be uplifted by all sorts of circumstances. When a new checkout line opens up at a crowded store and you happen to be in the right spot to be first in the new line, don't you feel good?

Or, when you lose a cell phone or cherished scarf and remember when you last had it and return to the location and find it waiting for you—don't you feel destined for good fortune?

Seeing my name on a sign that I pass every day at the beginning of what I want to think of as the **Year of Deb** is no small thing.

Grateful Dozen Category: What's so funny, Neighborhood discoveries, January 12, 2015

What Makes This Seder Different?

L AST FRIDAY, I attended a *seder*. A couple days before
then, I joked with friends that I was going to celebrate
the ritual dinner commemorating the Jews' exodus from
Egypt with *real Jews*.

Those who know me know I was raised as a *Lox'n Bagels Jew*—I identified with the culture but didn't speak Hebrew or was particularly observant of traditions. I had participated in seders before but expected one held in an Orthodox home would be a very different kind of experience.

The Hebrew word "seder" translates to "order." I was struck by how much my initial reaction to the special meal and self-conducted service felt anything but orderly.

One of the traditions is the asking of The Four Questions. This, in itself, is a bit of a puzzle.

There aren't actually four different questions. One question is asked four times and is given four different answers.

The question is: "What makes this night different from all other nights?"

I couldn't help but ask myself, "What makes this Seder different from all other Seders?"

The traditional question has different answers that all refer to escaping from bondage and enjoying the life of free men. My question, "What makes this Seder different from all other Seders?" has different answers but all seem to come back to my notion of "order."

After receiving the invitation, I asked my host when I should arrive. She told me that she lights candles at sunset and that her family starts the Seder about an hour afterwards.

I didn't know what to make of this information. I was expecting her to tell me a specific time, but this threw me off. Was I supposed to come for Sabbath candle lighting or just for dinner? Apparently, it was for me to decide.

The leader of the service didn't pass out copies of the same Haggadah to everyone as I was accustomed to, clearly marked with passages to be read by assigned individuals.

Haggadahs were distributed to anyone who wanted one, but there were maybe eight different versions. The idea was that you would pick out the translation that suited you and would follow the proceedings that way.

While there was a leader for the service, everyone was invited to contribute comments or questions, insights or observations.

As I looked around the room, everyone seemed to be doing their own thing.

The Seder leader read the text in Hebrew very quickly. My friend's father, affectionately referred to as Zadie by everyone (grandfather) sang songs of the holiday, not concerned with whether anyone was listening. Guests shared thoughts about writings that pertained to particular Passover traditions.

One of the children sitting at the head table, presented his understanding of the ten Plagues, which, according to the bible, was to demonstrate the power of God and persuade Pharaoh to let the Jews leave Egypt. He displayed representations of each plague, throwing fake lice and miniature frog-shaped toys across the room.

This Seder didn't look like *order* to me.

Then I looked at the room *from my heart*. Everyone had so much love and respect for each other. Everyone followed their inner guidance. We all probably took a few moments to silently gather our thoughts and form prayers about how we wanted to spend the holiday the following year.

Maybe that is the true meaning of why people celebrate the holiday. As free people, with faith in God and respect for others, we can create our own order—one that is satisfying for ourselves and encouraging to those we love.

Seeing twenty-five people sitting around a dining table, each following their own impulses and giving everyone else space to follow theirs is no small thing.

Grateful Dozen Category: Musings- Adventures with My Mind,
Something New, April 7, 2015

Day At the Museum

I HAD THE OPPORTUNITY to visit a few area museums recently. A day at the museum is a great way to stimulate your curiosity or to satisfy it.

Wandering through the exhibits can bring up thoughts you don't typically think about or can answer questions you've often wondered about.

At the Field Museum, I like walking through the Maori

meetinghouse. The structure was built in 1881 and was brought over from New Zealand.

I also like checking out the reconstructed skeletons of dinosaurs. I'll find myself thinking about how a Tyrannosaurus ate, how it walked, how it fought, and how it adapted (or didn't) over time.

At the Shedd Aquarium, like the groups of junior high children on field trips, I'll stare at the underwater serpents that occupy individual tanks and marvel at the replications of large environments.

They have a Caribbean Reef display and a three million gallon *Oceanarium* that simulates the marine life of the Pacific Northwest. In visiting the Shedd, you have the chance to visit the Seven Seas—all in one place.

It's easy to lose track of time at the Museum Of Science and Industry. It may be the most impressive science museum in the world. It's a great place for anyone interested in how things in the physical world work.

Even during crowded days at the museum, earphones and buttons that respond to personal prompts make the learning experience personalized and very interactive.

Also, they have amazing exhibits you can walk through. You can ride down a coal elevator and see how coal is extracted from the earth (a permanent exhibit since 1933). The museum also houses a World War II German submarine that was retrieved from the Atlantic.

There are exhibits about green energy and weather—you can actually see how a tsunami forms under water—and a wonderful exhibit about how humans develop, both physically and personality-wise. The space center has replicas of Apollo capsules and regularly shows 3-D movies.

My favorite exhibit at the MSI, though, is the model train in the main rotunda.

Twenty trains travel on over 1400 feet of track through constructed landscapes representing the Great Plains and the Rockies. The level of detail is incredible. Trains go over bridges, through mountains, past signals, and even switch tracks.

I could stare at the trains moving along their routes for ages. I especially like when a train picks up speed and then disappears into a tunnel burrowed into the side of a mountain. I'll often hold my breath when the front car vanishes from view until it re-emerges into the light.

I guess I'm more interested in the unseen than in easily observed phenomena. It seems that there are things we know to be true, but we can't always explain why, or we can't be sure someone else shares the same understanding.

I wish there was a Museum of Metaphysics and Experiential Understanding (MMEU). I wish there were simple interactive exercises so people could fully take in the Law of Attraction or Law of Cause and Effect.

Maybe life itself is like a day at the MMEU, although it would be nice if we learned more about how the universe operates as children and didn't spend so much of our lives unlearning limiting beliefs.

Every exhibit in every museum I've ever visited had something to teach me, but I especially love the lesson of the model train. Even though I've seen it dozens of times, the lesson always seems to be timely.

I love watching the train disappear in the side of the mountain, content knowing that even though I can't see its progress along the track, it will come out of the tunnel at the right time.

Like going through any transition in life, understanding that darkness is only temporary is no small thing.

Grateful Dozen Category: Musings—Adventures with
My Mind, April 27, 2015

Never Too Old

OR WEEKS BEFORE I left for Buenos Aires, I scanned *TripAdvisor* and old *Fodor's* and *Lonely Planet* guidebooks. I wanted to get ideas on what might be considered **must dos** in a limited amount of time.

Eating grass-fed beef and sampling the national cookie, the alfajor, quickly went on my **to do** list. Of course, I had to catch a tango show and check out a milonga.

Buenos Aires is also famous for their ferias, their outdoor markets. Anywhere from thirty to hundreds of stands can occupy a neighborhood square or blocks of continuous streets.

The vendors might feature bric-a-brac, like old silverware or colored glasses, or small leather goods. At some markets, you might find handmade silver jewelry and antiques.

After some research, I set my heart on going to the Feria de San Telmo, the largest market in town. It starts at the Plaza Dorrego and runs all the way up Defensa Street.

About 300 vendors show their wares each Sunday. Fortunately, the weather was good on the last Sunday of my stay, and I found a cab driver that understood my imperfect directions.

Before I even got to the square, I saw several photographers and artists that had set up shop. I wondered how they were ready to go to work before noon when they probably only got in from their Saturday night a few hours earlier.

I came to look more than to shop, but it was hard not to buy a few things. I treated myself to a couple black and white prints of bandoneons, accordions used to play tango music, and I bought myself a scarf.

At the San Telmo market, I saw everything from gaucho pants to old copper tea kettles to antique telephones to hand-drawn mandalas.

Entrepreneurial teenage boys wielded portable coffee shops (carts) down the brick road, serving croissants, coffee, and yerba mate (a hot tea-like infusion). One man, zigzagging down Defensa, looking like *Chicken Man,* sold feather dusters from a basket on his back.

On one corner of the square, in front of Brasserie Petanque, a fixture at the weekly fest, they laid down a ten foot square piece of wooden board. A few musicians gathered nearby and an old couple danced the tango.

A bucket was set out to collect donations. Who knows if the man and woman were husband and wife, or brother and sister, or just good dancers, but watching them triggered such a sweet sense of romance in me. And hopefulness. I watched them dance for some time.

They were graceful. They obviously felt the music. There was a clear affection and shared history between them. They loved dancing together.

It was a strange sort of intimacy displayed in public, natural and inspiring. More beautiful than the toned and precise dancers I saw at the Madero Tango show.

Dressing up and dancing in the square on Sunday afternoons was just what they did.

I thought . . .

You're never too old to fall in love.

You're never too old to dance in public.

You're never too old to put on a fedora or don your lowest hanging earrings.

You're never too old to hang out with the band.

You're never too old . . . .

My mind created a slew of ways to complete this sentence. It was nice to think about possibilities instead of limitations or excuses.

Not only did I get to see the merchants and shoppers at the Feria de San Telmo, I got to see the tango performed with unexpected tenderness and beauty.

Believing that I, too, can radiate love and vitality as I age, is no small thing.

Grateful Dozen Category: Beauty,
September 7, 2015

Do Argentine Pigeons Tango?

MY ARRIVAL AT EZE, the international airport of Buenos Aires, was E-A-S-Y.

The driver that was arranged to pick me up arrived on time. Sporting a mustachioed smile, I spotted him holding a hand-lettered sign with my name just beyond the automatic glass doors past the baggage claim.

He didn't speak much English and I spoke even less Spanish. He laughed when I demonstrated the limits of my vocabulary: *cerveza fria, vino tinto, la cuenta, hola,* and *el bano.*

Getting to my hotel too early for check-in, I decided to take a short walking tour of the immediate area. I wandered through the famous cemetery where *Don't Cry For Me Argentina* Evita is buried. I made a mental note not to bother to visit the ubiquitous Irish bar and Hard Rock Café that was also nearby.

Within a couple minutes, I found myself at the Museo Nacional de Bellas Artes; a wonderful FREE museum featuring works by Van Gogh, Degas, Gauguin, and Modigliani.

After the museum, it dawned on me that I hadn't eaten anything except airplane food for about twenty-four hours. I was an *easy* target for the hostess of a restaurant/bar a few doors from my hotel. She was trying to entice passersby to take advantage of their prix fixe lunch special.

I sat at a table outside and enjoyed a leisurely lunch consisting of an empanada appetizer, a grilled sirloin steak, yummy profiteroles, and a fine glass of Malbec. All for about twenty dollars!

As I was finishing, at around 3:00, the lunch crowd was just starting to fill up the café seats. In Argentina, dinner is normally eaten at around 10:00 or 11:00, and lunch is taken long past mid-day.

Sipping my wine, I became transfixed and amused by the sight of pigeons venturing boldly near the tables.

One pigeon, maybe Francisco or Christina Maria, strutted between the tables as if she owned the place. The bird did not seem bothered by either the tourists nor the narrowness of the path between tables. While wide in the chest, this bird looked almost delicate and deliberate in her movements.

I had to ask myself, *Do Argentinian pigeons tango?*

Do Argentinian pigeons step lightly?

Do they walk in straight lines and move with their flock in an oval?

Can they walk backwards?

Do they look for partners?

Can they execute an ocho, pivoting on the balls of their feet, their claws?

Do they attempt an occasional scissors kick when they feel like showing off?

Do they listen to an inner music and synchronize their movements to the beats of their hearts?

We have pigeons in Chicago. I mostly think of them as a nuisance, as poor-flying birds and virtual shitting machines. (Is any statue, plaza, or church steeple safe from their droppings?)

I normally don't wax on romantically about pigeons. I don't usually think about them in magical, almost human terms. I was surprised that under the umbrella of my little table in a Recoleta cafe, with a near empty-glass of vino tinto, I couldn't take my eyes off them.

But maybe this shouldn't come as a surprise.

That a traveler can look at something very common from a different vantage point, feeding their imagination and stirring up a sense of wonder, is no small thing.

Grateful Dozen Category: Tourist Eyes,
August 20, 2015

Dress Rehearsal

I GOT TO MY seat just before the lights dimmed and the *announcement* was made.

Before any overture, Roger Pines, the dramaturg at the Lyric Opera, or some other nicely suited gentleman, walks onto the stage and reminds people that they are about the see a ***dress rehearsal.***

He politely points out that the performers might not choose to sing in full voice and that the production could be stopped, at the director's discretion, to fix or change things.

I've seen many dress rehearsals over the years. I've noticed occasions when the crew will probably work on picking up the pace for scene changes, but I've never seen a performance stopped and divas or star baritones asked for a *do-over*.

For the most part, dress rehearsals are as good as performances staged during the official run. In some ways, they're better.

Before I grabbed a program and journeyed up the aisle to my seat, I remembered the sights of the grand hall.

There were couples with young children, maybe eight to twelve years old. The kids, dressed in their Sunday clothes for an afternoon outing downtown, fidgeted with excitement.

A caped woman (no, not really a superhero) scanned their tickets. I tried to imagine their reaction to things inside the auditorium. It holds 3,500 and the ceiling is finished in gold leaf.

Not what they'd see at the local Cineplex.

While I wondered if their parents would be asked to explain the bawdy parts in their SUV during their ride home, I liked to think that, for a ten year-old, of *The Marriage of Figaro* is a wonderful introduction to opera.

I liked the idea that this matinee at the civic opera house welcomed a good percentage of first timers. Certainly, most of the audience, which represented nearly a full house, were *gifted* their tickets.

Dress rehearsal tickets at the Lyric are considered donor benefits. Most of my fellow audience members got passes from someone they knew who was a season subscriber or donor.

I am the happy benefactor of four dress rehearsal tickets for this season from my sister who has been a subscriber for a gazillion years.

Dress rehearsal tickets are free! Either a subscriber uses her allotment because she gets a special pleasure from comparing this performance to one from the middle of the run or she gives the ticket to someone she knows who really, really wants to go.

Maybe she has a friend who can't afford a ticket or maybe knows someone who is just interested in certain operas and not in subscribing for the season.

As I contemplated what was different about this production from other productions of Figaro that I've seen, I contemplated this as well: the audience was so **happy** to be here.

I think I prefer going to preview nights of plays as well.

Maybe performers love opening nights the most. They enjoy the buzz around a new production, having family members in the audience, or the chance that a critic will see them and speak well of them in reviews.

Maybe the box office and board members beam at the prospects of a sell-out. For Friday and Saturday night performances, the valet attendants might take special care to service VIPs and nearby eateries are happy to take early dinner reservations.

But I think I like going to dress rehearsals the best because most audience members are experiencing the performance as a **gift**.

Being around the energy of appreciation is no small thing.

Grateful Dozen Category: Musings—Adventures with my Mind, Feeling Like a Winner, October 5, 2015

Resting Place

A s I WAS driving along Montrose the other day, I saw what looked like a bird convention.

Flocks seemed to break out of formation and seek out every available inch on nearby streetlamps and the roof cornice of Jeri's Grill, and I don't think they were lining up for a booth or were interested in sampling their biscuits and gravy.

I had to pull over and watch them for a few minutes. I kept thinking about the line from the Robert Frost poem, "... *And miles to go before I sleep,*" from "Stopping by Woods on a Snowy Evening."

These birds were flying south for the winter. A long journey, but one that they were compelled to take each year. No need for GPS or special navigational device. Maybe they knew the direction from the feel of the sun on their backs.

And just as certainly, they knew when to take advantage of a resting spot.

I used to hang out by the Lincoln Park lagoon in the fall and marvel at the sight of Canadian geese flying in V-formations. Hard to believe the same birds that seemed so oddly proportioned and awkward on their feet could look so elegant in flight.

The birds hanging out at Jeri's roof were smaller and more mundane. Their flight path, while maybe not as long or constrained by the shape they took for group flight, was challenging because of the sheer size of their group.

I wondered if the same group stayed together for their entire journey or if individual birds naturally broke away from one flock and reattached to another after resting, when ready to move again. Anyway, there must have been over thirty.

I thought about summer vacations when I was growing up, road trips to the Wisconsin Dells or South Haven, Michigan. My father would often pull off the highway at a rest stop, even when we didn't need gas.

Rest stops usually included toilets and vending machines and often included a place to eat and a gift shop.

Before these roadside oases featured familiar fast food franchises like Subway, our favorite place to stop was Stuckeys. My sisters and I could get lost wandering through the gift shop. We would invariably bring pecan divinities or log rolls back to the car, making the next leg of our trip messier but oh-so-much sweeter.

It's amazing how many rest stops cross my path in any day. I don't usually give their presence much thought.

At large indoor shopping malls, there are atriums with greenery (even plastic greenery can be welcome after staring at modern Plexiglass displays). When you need to suspend exercising your credit card—which we all know, can be exhausting—you can head to the food court and sit down.

There are usually coffee shops by commuter stations. Fitting that places where people are on the go are surrounded by places made for stopping.

There are also benches by bus stops, alongside walking paths, or overlooking scenic views. I thought of this phenomena as a little miracle as I watched the migrating birds on the roof of Jeri's Grill.

It must be an overlooked law of nature that usually when you have to rest, the perfect resting spot appears, or maybe when you need to take five or ten, any place you stop seems like the perfect spot.

Appreciating welcoming places to rest and taking the time to give yourself a break is no small thing.

Grateful Dozen Category: Neighborhood Discoveries, Noticing Small Things, November 9, 2015

Collective Memories

"H E WAS A legend," John pulled me under his arm and pointed to a mountain of a man, a *mountain man* type of man sporting salt and pepper colored facial hair and more than a few extra inches around his waist. "He started this bar thirty years ago. He brought in bottled imports. No one did that back then," John went on. "He's a legend."

Everyone at the gathering was a *legend, at least* in the eyes of everyone else there. And there were stories to tell!

Around twenty-five characters gathered at _____ to see a good friend who, fighting the effects of glioblastoma and the prescribed treatments, had to work hard to organize his

Deborah Hawkins

memories of the world they shared together. They also came to breathe life into their own memories.

To them, _____ was a place where everyone knew your name, like in the long-running TV show Cheers.

As part-time bartenders, or like Norm and postman Cliff Clavin, full-time bar stool *sitters*, they spent most Thursday evenings together drinking and obsessing over their fantasy baseball league. This was thirty years ago, back when stats weren't managed automatically on laptops or Smartphones.

I wasn't part of this crowd, but it was so easy talking to everyone now. I just had to explain the nexus of connections and I was in. I relayed how I came with John who bartended with Steve back in 1980-something.

Then somebody would invariably tell me about a secret crush they had on John or about how they went on a ridiculously long motorcycle adventure with someone else I knew. Suddenly, it was as if we were related.

My father used to call this *Jewish Geography*, how if you talk to people with the intention of finding out what you have in common or who you both know, you invariably find out you do have something or someone in common. If it's not already a small world, a healthy dose of *small talk* renders it one.

I had never met Steve before this week, except on the phone and through his blog, My Big Fat Greek Cancer. I knew he loved Beat Generation writers, his wife and daughter—and, oh yes, the Cubs. And we all know how frustrating that love affair can be.

Oddly, I felt very close to him during this reunion. Albeit for our own reasons, we were both putting our whole hearts and minds into making sense of how people were connected.

At one point, he came up to me and apologized that he couldn't speak to me more personally at such a gathering. It was too crowded. The bar was too noisy. There were too many distractions.

Moments later, he excused himself because he spotted three other people he wanted to swap stories with. It was not a time for deep conversations but for deep recognition of belonging.

The afternoon unfolded as it unfolded. I was glad to be a part of it.

A fine bottle of Monkey Shoulders Scotch was divvied up in plastic cups for a ceremonial toast. I think this is how a group hug is performed at _____. Promises to get together, aside from such occasions, were exchanged. People showed off pictures of their children on their cell phones.

I think Steve was genuinely touched by the experience. Of course, I went on a philosophical jag.

The present moment belongs to no one. Memories of our lives, the facts and fictions we've adopted, belong to everyone we touch. Memories can be deeply personal, but the truth of a human life is too important to leave in the hands of one person.

We all are here to remember **for each other**. Only together, can we get close to the truth of our stories—and that's no small thing.

Grateful Dozen Category: Belonging,
June 24, 2016

Redemption

W HAT COULD BE more American than the Fourth of July (besides guns and monster trucks)?
Baseball.

During my trip to Greenville, South Carolina, it wasn't surprising to discover they had a minor league team, a farm team for the Boston Red Sox. What I didn't know until I perused my hotel's *What to Do In Greenville* magazine, was that Pickens County was the home of **Shoeless Joe Jackson**.

Baseball . . . Chicago connection . . . I felt charged with the mission of visiting his modest home, now a folksy sort of mini-museum, relocated across the street from where The Drive play in a replica of Fenway Park; Green Monster left field wall and all.

They offered free tours of the house given by a volunteer docent: a fit elderly gentleman with a great memory for facts and an even greater appreciation for the extraordinary life and character of Greenville's favorite son.

Walking up the few steps, then through the doorway of this modest home, I was quickly bathed in cool, air-conditioned air. Beyond being a repository for memorabilia and a retail outlet for Shoeless Joe tees, coffee mugs and baseball caps, the tiny residence served as a welcome refuge on this muggy June afternoon.

The docent greeted visitors and asked where we were from. Then he pointed out Joe as a young player from a selection of team photos that hung on a nearby wall.

He handed us tri-fold cream colored brochures that captured most of the factoids, but I couldn't take my attention away from him. His words spilled out like a testimonial from a faithful friend.

I knew that Joe Jackson—who, we were told, hated the nickname *Shoeless Joe*—was supposed to have remarkable baseball skills, but he sounded positively Paul Bunyan-esque.

From a poor, rural family, he went to work for a local mill, sweeping the cotton dust off the floor at six. By thirteen, he was playing baseball for their company team and was such a noticeable talent, his brothers used to try collecting tips from people who came to watch him play.

From his position in left field, he could throw the ball 400 feet to home plate where the runner could be tagged OUT, all without a single bounce.

He batted .408 his rookie year (1911), the highest batting average claimed by a rookie. He finished his short-lived career with a batting average of .356, the third highest in baseball history.

Our guide set a little backdrop for the story of the 1919 scandal, the year Chicago's south side team was called the Black Sox.

The sport of baseball was slanted a lot to benefit the owners. Many took advantage of their players. Owner of the White Sox, Charles Comiskey, was known to be especially cheap.

According to our guide, some of Joe's teammates wanted to enlist Joe in a scam to throw the World Series, for which they were heavy favorites, so that they could make some money from bookies.

That star players could make more money from this scheme than they could from their salaries or endorsements reflects the huge change in the economics of sports.

The docent's voice was unwavering as he told the rest of the story; how Joe Jackson refused to be in on the scheme, how his performance for the series (twelve hits and no errors on defense) was not one that reflected anything but a desire to win; how the group of players were acquitted.

But Joe Jackson and seven of his teammates were banished from baseball to send a no-tolerance message.

Joe and his wife Kate moved to Savannah, Georgia then back to South Carolina. They ran different businesses and led a comfortable life . . . but he couldn't finish his baseball career.

He defended himself in the press and in person. He lived the remainder of his life with a clear conscience. And I couldn't help but feel that, although baseball, didn't reinstate him, his innocence and undeniable talent is kept alive by the people that believed him.

As I stood in his parlor in front of his favorite bat, Black Betsy, and radio, I felt his presence. I felt that he was at peace.

He spoke his truth and the sons of his neighbors still think of him as a kind man and incredible athlete.

I think that somehow he was redeemed by the faith of Greenville.

Today is the Fourth of July, and I've been thinking about this encounter with the spirit of Joe Jackson.

I've been thinking that our national celebration is as much about the possibility for *Redemption* as it is about *independence*.

It seems important to Americans to remember the spirit of unsurpassed potential this country was born with and, not withstanding our many failings, embrace our potential as our guide in moving forward.

Believing that you can live up to your promise is no small (American) thing.

Grateful Dozen Category: Tourist Eyes,
July 4, 2016

Beneath the Windshield

I JUST CAME HOME from a whirlwind excursion.

I drove to Madison, Wisconsin for a family event, leaving Friday afternoon to drive back home on Sunday.

It's about 150 miles one-way, but it can be driven in two and a half hours if you don't encounter construction or traffic, but as that's pretty unlikely, it usually takes closer to three.

I considered having a good stretch of time behind the wheel, behind the windshield. Just the word itself makes you feel protected in your moving bubble. Like an Arthurian knight, all will be well behind your windshield.

I rarely take on an uninterrupted stretch of highway driving these days.

I helped a friend move to a new home in Arkansas some years ago where I drove twelve hours straight through. For four consecutive summers, I drove to a retreat in upstate New York, and I went on a couple fabulous Canadian driving vacations. One took me through the Canadian Rockies and the other through the Laurentian mountain range.

The longest road trip I took was when I helped another friend move from Chicago to Sonoma, California. She hired professional movers for hauling furniture, but our mission was to bring her German Shepard, Jack, and her husband's BMW out there.

Jack was full of anxiety and shed hair like crazy as he curled up in a sort of hammock we arranged in the back seat. We drove for four days, through the flat lands of Nebraska, following the tumbling tumbleweeds of Wyoming, and silently prayed to ourselves that the wind tunnel created to make a path through the Sierra Nevada range didn't suck us into some unknown vortex.

I have learned from past road trips that it's good to bring some music. Being from a generation where that didn't mean cueing up a playlist from my smartphone, I had set aside a few CDs . . . but I forgot them.

Playing music and watching the world from my driver's seat can provide a lot of pleasure. It represents quality ALONE TIME. I feel in control. Safe. Constantly entertained by the changing scenery all around me.

But because I didn't have my planned music with me, I decided to make friends with my car radio—just beneath my window to the world.

I was able to get a favorite FM station from Chicago until I caught sight of the Chrysler assembly plant in Belvidere, Illinois. At over five million square feet, I reflected how workers there might be extra careful not to leave their cell phone or lunch in their cars, not having the time to go to the parking lot and retrieve them.

At this point, I pushed my index finger against the radio's SEARCH button. I came up with a rock station (WXRX), which I listened to until static replaced the recognizable guitar riffs.

Between Belvidere and Madison—where there are plenty of music choices catering to state university students—I caught signals for Country (WXXQ) out of Freeport and Classic Rock from Sauk City, Wisconsin (WIBA). I even got signals from a Hip-Hop station out of Genoa, Illinois (WYRB). *Who knew?*

I was tickled by how my SEARCH button would lead me to music I wouldn't know to look for. I quickly moved on when I locked in to a religious station's signal, and there are plenty of them across this country.

I got a strange idea in my head. What if everyone was equipped with a sort of SEARCH button? I contemplated how wonderful it would be, when not consciously directed to something, if you could press a button and pick up compatible signals (people or jobs or activities) to engage with until you were aware of a passion to move towards.

I hadn't reached Janesville yet, and I was laughing out loud, delighted by my own thoughts.

I looked through my windshield. I thought about the trucks and SUVs that had passed me miles ago that I was passing now. I noticed that the block of clouds that had been hanging over the highway had moved on. I smiled at how signs for different gas brands were built extra high so from a distance drivers could see them and plot out which exit they should take.

Recognizing that life itself and my imagination can provide an endless stream of ideas sparked a sort of contentment.

Believing in your own capacity to never get bored is no small thing.

Grateful Dozen Category: Self-Appreciation, Musings—
Adventures with My Mind, August 20, 2016

Remembering
the Words

ONE OF MY priorities for my trip to Portugal was to hear
Fado as often as possible.

Popularized in the early twentieth century in Lisbon,
Fado songs can be about anything but are usually composed in
minor keys and capture a feeling of longing.

There are contemporary Fado singers, fadistas, and songs
can be performed with accompaniment or not. Remarkably,
even rock star, slickly produced performers, take the tradition
seriously.

There's a sort of universality and timelessness about a man or woman capturing their yearnings in a song.

On my first night in Lisbon while walking around the Alfama, a man, who was promoting a restaurant and club, approached us. After listening to his pitch, Midwestern skeptics that we were, we excused ourselves and walked on.

Not having a better idea where to go, we came back and let him lead us to a small restaurant and club down a narrow street just off the main drag.

They had a limited menu, although very good cod (the specialty of the region), and they served food and drink in between short sets. Four different fadistas visited the club during the evening and sang a selection of songs which were accompanied by two house guitarists. They then went to other supper clubs where, I assume, they did the same.

We went to another supper club two days later, in the Chiado district, where the food and music were higher quality, and set at a much higher cost.

A couple days later, we were in Coimbra, where I had been forewarned that Fado was different than it was in Lisbon. Following their local tradition, where Fado was sung by male university students to the women they wanted to woo, only men sang.

After catching touristy shows at Casa de Fado and Fado ao Centro, at a local diner where we lunched on piglet and potato chips, we were directed to visit Bar Diligencia (which roughly translates to stagecoach).

No cover charge. Cheap drinks. No one shows up until 10:00. Ah, the real deal!

The singer, a bearded young man, who looked like he could have been a college student anywhere in the world, sat on a chair and alternated between two different guitars. There were only about eight people in the bar. The manager spoke good English and was very welcoming.

The Fadista sang a few traditional tunes, in between which, he asked members of his audience where they were from. Although our shoes probably gave our origin away, he seemed happy when we said *Chicago*, the *U.S.*

In his second set, he asked the audience if we knew **Pink Floyd**. Well, of course. I was surprised by the question. What did Pink Floyd have to do with Fado? I expected that he was preparing us for an audience participation bit in the song, but I didn't know what song he was preparing us for.

Then he tore into the most beautiful acoustic version of "Wish You Were Here" that I had ever heard. Then it dawned on me.

What could capture the spirit of Fado more? What song could top this one for expressing pure longing? "WISH YOU WERE HERE . . ."

I considered my own longings. It seems that I've spent most of my life trying to find my voice—to find an audience and be heard. I've looked for opportunities to make my feelings known through writing.

But many times, I've had problems speaking up within relationships. When given the opportunity to make a point in a discussion, I often can't get the words out. I've been afraid of saying things wrong or of not being understood.

And here I was at Bar Diligencia, a tavern in Coimbra, Portugal, and I knew what was coming. Although I would never see anyone else in the audience again, I knew that the singer would lead everyone up to a certain point in the lyrics and go silent expecting everyone who knew Pink Floyd would take over.

For a few moments, I worried if I'd remember the words,

but when the performer stopped singing and played guitar for everyone else to fill in the words, I belted out the phrase.

"*Like two lost souls swimming in a fishbowl—year after year.*"

Wow, I felt like a fadista. Suddenly, I was unafraid of my longing to be heard. In fact, it was celebrated. It was shared.

Remembering the words to a song and giving those words voice is no small thing.

Grateful Dozen Category: Belonging, Self-Appreciation,
November 7, 2016

Midnight Circus

L IGHT AND FLUFFY snowflakes are coming down. I hear the sound of my neighbor running a shovel blade across the walk. I have food in the fridge and nowhere I have to be.

Here, at home, life seems very peaceful. Inside the snow globe, the movements of the world seem like MAGIC.

At this time of year, TV commercials show new luxury cars

tied up in red bows sitting on suburban driveways, sending sparks of glee to the lucky family who unties the ribbon and enjoys keyless entry and being the envy of their neighbors (at low monthly rates).

This image is supposed to convey the MAGIC of the season.

But I have another recent memory of magic, one that is far simpler and feels truer.

Back in October, I went to see The Midnight Circus, at nearby Welles Park. During the summer months, The Chicago Shakespeare Theatre stages productions of the Bard's works in neighborhood parks.

During September and October, The Midnight Circus sets up its tent, and parks its popcorn machine in many of the same parks.

I have had no recent experience of going to the circus. I remember when I was around four, my father pulled some strings to get front row seats to the Ringling Brothers Circus.

My sister, who was only one year older, and I got upset and scared by the humongous elephants. And when the clowns (face it, clowns are pretty scary) pulled a stunt where they pretended to set their hair on fire—well, we screamed so loudly that our poor father had to take us home.

The Midnight Circus was a much tamer affair. The largest animals they had were dogs no bigger than a Cocker Doodle. There was a high wire act, but the wire was about as high as a basketball net.

The circus troop, mostly acrobats and jugglers, was composed of young people, spanning in age from ten to twenty-five. They wore tight fitting and colorful outfits and moved with energy and grace.

Although comic bits were performed, thankfully, there were no scary clowns.

A very eclectic range of music was amplified and, except for one intermission, there was no stoppage. I watched a constant flow of acts.

A young girl dangled from the top of the tent on a large swatch of purple cloth, arranging her Gumby doll-like body into configurations I didn't think possible.

A teenage couple leapt and danced across a wire, stepping through hoops and tossing each other different objects from opposite ends.

Two hours of non-stop entertainment. In my little neighborhood. UNDER THE BIG TOP.

I enjoyed the skill and simple beauty of human bodies in motion, but there was another element that was MAGICAL to me.

As I looked around the crowd, maybe around three hundred in total, everybody's eyes were on the performers. There were families with young children and twenty-somethings on dates. All ages were represented. Nowhere did I see the glow of a smart phone.

This shouldn't be so rare, but I've been to too many concerts and too many nice restaurants where it seemed that the main attraction was texting cryptic conversations with people who were not around.

Here, people were sharing an actual experience in real time. They were seeing the same thing at the same time and fed off of everyone else's awe and delight.

Seeing everyone together under the big top. To me, this was magic.

Enjoying entertainment with friends and neighbors—in the moment—is no small thing.

Grateful Dozen Category: Neighborhood Discoveries,
Something New, December 19, 2016

Mud

IT MUST HAVE rained for two days straight. At times, the raindrops pelted down, sounding of tin against my windows. Even when drops didn't come down as discrete objects, a heavy mist permeated the air.

There wasn't a sidewalk that didn't end at the nearest street in lake-sized puddles. Even walking to the parking pad behind my building involved planning where I planted each footstep.

I hung an old gray towel in the entryway to my building, acknowledging that it would be necessary to clean India's paws after returning from a walk.

Mud was everywhere.

I noticed how I became fascinated with this; how I looked for paw prints or patterned treads from boots in splashes of mud I'd encountered on the sidewalk.

I noticed that where small bites of earth had been pulled away from itself, exposed dirt became dry sooner than in places where larger craters had been scooped out.

I noticed discarded cans, candy wrappers, and small branches stuck in the mud. It seemed that people were much less apt to clear these things out of the way. An expedition to pick up incidental refuse would surely lead to messing up your shoes.

Mud is innocuous enough when you think about its composition. It's just earth and water. But it carries its own unique danger. It marks anything that comes close. Upon contact, it defines what it touches. Things become muddy.

It's a symbol, of sorts, of gluttony. When I see mud in abundance, I think about how a lawn or garden is trying to take in more water than it can swallow and absorb.

I told my friend Carol about my recent fixation and she remarked that according to Buddhist and Eastern traditions, it's important to remember that mud is the environment where the lotus flower grows.

As I've been discouraged by many of the recent political and social trends, I've tried to keep in mind that a certain level of messiness is necessary for positive change to take place.

In my own creative process, I've recognized that sometimes ideas can seem very disconnected and raw before I can put them together in any way that approaches coherence (let alone the honesty and elegance I might strive for).

But this was a notion worth taking in—that something as beautiful as the lotus flower *grows* in the mud. Like a baby chick cracking its shell from the inside, the implication is that there's a certain amount of effort necessary for something so beautiful to be born.

Life itself is **mud**. There are things that are unavoidable. It's messy. And the tension itself, the struggle involved in surviving and reaching out, on its own, creates a certain kind of beauty.

Just last week, I heard that someone I had worked with a few years ago died of breast cancer. I learned that I would get a tax refund this year. One of my projects got postponed and I might not have income for a couple weeks. A friend comp-ed me with a ticket to the symphony. I was complimented and criticized.

Thupten Ngodrup, the State Oracle of Tibet, in sharing his thoughts on the lotus, said,

"The lotus is the most beautiful flower, whose petals open one by one. But it will only grow in the mud. In order to grow and gain wisdom, first you must have the mud —- the obstacles of life and its suffering. . . . The mud speaks of the common ground that humans share, no matter what our stations in life. . . . Whether we have it all or we have nothing, we are all faced with the same obstacles: sadness, loss, illness, dying and death. If we are to strive as human beings to gain more wisdom, more kindness and more compassion, we must have the intention to grow as a lotus and open each petal one by one."

Celebrating **MUD** is no small thing.

Grateful Dozen Category: Beauty, Musings—Adventures with My Mind, April 3, 2017

Garden Off Edens

THE CHICAGO BOTANIC Garden is not in Chicago. It's actually in a suburb called Glencoe, just off the Edens Expressway about twenty miles north.

Arranging a lunch date with a friend, who lives in a suburb close to the Wisconsin border, provided an excuse for making the garden a destination this past Friday afternoon.

They have a very nice cafeteria, six parking lots—which actually fill completely during the summer months—and constantly changing natural beauty.

At the front of the visitors center, there is a *What's in Bloom* display and a large-scale map of the nearly 400 acre garden. Although there are plenty of maps and trail markers throughout, I usually just wander down the paths and focus on what's in front of me (until I want to return to the parking lot).

When I visited on Friday, I read the *What's in Bloom* cards that greeted me at the front of the building. If I couldn't tell already from the colorful blooms I saw on the way in from the Lake Cook Road entrance, after checking out the display, I knew to be prepared to see rhododendrons, magnolias, and tulips.

"When did this happen?" I remember saying to myself earlier in the week as I was driving home via the Wilson Avenue Bridge.

It seems that my neighborhood came to life overnight. Last Saturday, things were subdued. By Thursday, I saw a broad palette of greens and pinks from budding trees. (Based on the name, who'd think a crabapple tree would be so beautiful?)

I felt like Dorothy from the *Wizard of Oz* when she first opened the door of Auntie Em's and Uncle Henry's cabin after her jarring trip and landing over the rainbow. Everything went from shades of gray to technicolor. It seemed that the landscape and sense of life happening around me turned just as quickly.

I'll often find things especially beautiful based on the surprise element. I'll stop in amazement at the sight of a flower daring to break through the ground at a construction site or a child's smile caught as I look at the car next to mine while stopped at a traffic light.

But visiting CBG was a different experience of beauty. Flowers and shrubs and trees are always beautiful but being able to walk for hours without the distractions of car horns or technology put me in a state of mind where I'm relaxed and can BE with everything.

I felt elevated. The recognition itself, that a garden is a **special** place, was beautiful. What came over me seemed inescapable in such a large wonderland of nature, but I think this is true of smaller gardens as well.

A garden doesn't just happen. It has to be tended.

Over weeks, months, even years, someone thinks of how to use an outdoor space. Seeds are chosen and planted. Soil and rocks and fertilizer and planters may be bought. Someone spends time on their knees making sure the soil is soft and there are no weeds or other things that might challenge a plant.

From March through October, I'll often see my building neighbor Paula on her knees with a spade in her hand.

I'm always delighted when I see the row of hostas between our building and the brick of the building next to ours. I love seeing the small trees she planted along the wire fence that provides a barrier to the Brown Line tracks just a few feet beyond my back deck.

I know she considers what types of plants need sunlight or shade before seeds are put in the ground. She always makes arrangements for Alisa or Grant or me to water everything when she goes out of town. I'll take note of her many runs to Home Depot's Garden Center.

And the Chicago Botanic Garden must have armies of Paulas; keeping their incredible collection of Bonsai trees trimmed and in proportion, keeping their lawns pristine, placing benches in the walled garden so that you can enjoy the trees and blooms in private while dozens of other visitors are doing the same, planning where to arrange different varieties of rose bushes so that when their time comes in June, you can't help but be bowled over.

Having a special appreciation for a place where the finest expression of the natural world meets the care and stewardship of human beings is no small thing.

Grateful Dozen Category: Beauty, April 24, 2017

Blue Skies

OH MY GOD.

When I headed out to walk India the other morning, I was amazed by the blueness of the sky.

Chicago is not known for its sunny days, but sometimes, you don't realize how wonderful something is—until you miss it.

Even though this winter has not been unduly harsh in temperature, after a chain of overcast days, I couldn't help but notice how different my mood was when I felt directly connected to the sun, under a cover of blue. A few wisps of clouds only added to the blessing by establishing a little contrast.

I felt more energetic and optimistic. I found myself more

willing to be spontaneous and adventurous. I seemed content to be alone, less eager for the distraction of a television or computer screen.

Even if I didn't want to be outside, I didn't want to lose sight of the amazing blue sky.

I think other people felt the same way.

In short interactions with store clerks or crossing guards or doormen, they all seemed especially upbeat and helpful.

It's not just the sunshine that people respond to. I'm convinced that it's the color blue itself. Indigo, periwinkle, cobalt, sapphire—there are many shades of blue in the spectrum. Everyone knows what SKY BLUE looks like.

I noodled around online for qualities and psychological associations with the color.

Peace
Calm
Clarity
Relaxation
Intelligence
Compassion
Spirituality
Sincerity
Flexibility
Imagination

It has been said that the color represents confidence, in a non-threatening way, as in CALM AUTHORITY.

The color is also associated with safety and trust.

It is universally liked. There are people whose favorite color might be red or green and other people who might be just as passionate in their dislike, but no one *hates* blue. It is universally liked.

I tried to understand the effect of the blue sky on my own mood and outlook. I had to think about horizons, and how the blueness of the ocean merges with the sky. Or, if you see a mountain, the only thing bigger is the sky over it.

When I see blue, I think FOREVER. INFINITY. Rather than being overwhelmed by this, I feel comforted.

I have to refer to the classic tune. (Thanks, Mr. Berlin)

Blue skies smilin' at me
Nothing but blue skies, do I see
Blue days all of them gone
Nothin' but blue skies from now on . . .

Being buoyed by the vastness, the FOREVER-NESS of the sky is no small thing.

Grateful Dozen Category:
Beauty, Musings—Adventures with my Mind,
February 7, 2017

I Want to Be a
Flamenco Dancer

ON THURSDAY EVENINGS during the summer, the North
Center and Lincoln Square Chamber of Commerce
sponsors free outdoor concerts in the plaza between
Café Selmarie and the new sandwich shop.

They feature a pretty eclectic sampling of musical genres,

from Peruvian folk music to American swing and a popular Beatles tribute band worked into the mix.

I have enjoyed going for years. I'll bring a lightweight-folding chair (stored in my car's trunk and ready for any bring-your-own-chair type of event) and will usually buy something to eat or drink there. The nearby Brauhaus restaurant sells very authentic veal brats from a kiosk in front of their door.

My experience of this summertime staple has waned a bit because the demographics of my neighborhood have changed.

Instead of old Germans who wish to be by their social clubs and young working professionals who want to be near public transportation, many young families have started to call this neighborhood HOME.

I don't know if there are actually more kids under five in the 'hood or if younger parents don't reign in their kids as parents did when I was growing up, but there is an amazing number of young children running around at these concerts.

The boys will often flash long balloon versions of Darth Vader swords and the girls will dance in their grandmothers' hippie beads while wearing several shades of purple.

While I don't want to come down on music lovers and summertime revelers, of any age, the atmosphere, reminiscent of a daycare center right before nap time, can make it harder to focus on the performance.

Just the other week, I got there early so I could stake out a spot near the small stage to see the Martin Metzger Flamenco Ensemble. The group consisted of a guitarist, a percussionist, a singer, and a dancer.

Decked out in a floor-length form-fitting skirt, hair dramatically pulled away from her face, the dancer miraculously handled a few costume changes during the evening.

Very quickly, I lost my primo view to kids that saw the open space in front of the stage as a good spot for dancing and running around and to millennials that decided to put their chairs right in front of mine.

The dialog in my head kicked in about this generation: how they move through the world with their ear buds in and their handheld devices on, how they seem single-minded in their focus on their personal agenda, how it seems that the rest of the world is INVISIBLE to them.

The volume of their conversations was high. It was as if they thought of the fine guitarist and singer as background sounds to their banter, not that their socializing was background to a performance. Between the rambunctious play of the children and self-absorbed audience members, I wondered how the musicians were able to concentrate.

I was copping a fowl mood.

Then I saw a little girl standing in front of the stage. Her gaze was transfixed on the dancer.

It was obvious that she had seen flamenco before and that it fascinated her. She wore a red and white ruffled dress and red shoes with a slightly elevated heel. Flamenco dancing shoes. She might not be ready to execute all the steps yet, but she was ready to look the part.

When the group's dancer did a combination of moves, upright yet graceful in her posture, her legs moving quickly, the insides of her feet almost touching, the little girl mimicked her. Or, at least, she got the stomping part down.

I could almost imagine the thoughts in the young girl's head.

"I want to be a flamenco dancer."

"I want to be beautiful but I also want to make noise. I want to be noticed."

"I want to honor those before me, those who teach me, but I also want to express myself in my own way."

For me, this image seemed to capture decisive moments of all kinds. Whether a person is choosing a career or place to live or someone to love. We can go through exercises of logic when coming to a decision, but ultimately the heart decides. And it decides in a moment.

Seeing this girl enthralled by the dancer only a few feet away kept my mind from going down the rabbit hole of dwelling on small annoyances.

That an image (and your awareness of its personal meaning) can turn your mood around is no small thing.

Grateful Dozen Category, Beauty, Neighborhood Discoveries,
July 11, 2017

New Day

I HAVE LEARNED SO much since India has come to live with me, just over three months ago.

She's an undetermined type of spaniel and poodle mix (a Spoodle?), mostly black with a white chest and belly and white tipped paws and center stripe along her snout. She's between a year and two years old.

She's about twenty-three pounds. Curious and affectionate, very good with people and other dogs. She'll be single-minded if she sees a squirrel she wants to chase, but has the sweetest temperament.

Of course, there's the obvious ways she has brought change into my life.

I have a greater appreciation for routine. Not that I don't enjoy a spontaneous adventure, but there's something very grounding about having breakfast, or maybe a walk, at about the same time each day.

Actually, having time slots already designated for certain activities is sort of liberating. As any day goes on, I already know what time I can use for new activities. I plan better. I don't feel rushed as often.

I have made a better habit of getting up and stretching. I have a greater respect for play.

It used to be automatic to sit at my desk all day, talking on the phone or eyes locked on my computer monitor. Now, upon seeing India curled up on her blanket in the corner of my office, and I'll take breaks more often.

We'll play fetch with a small green rubber ball down the long hallway of my apartment.

Watching her slide on my hardwood floors, in hot pursuit of the ball, always makes me smile.

She reminds me that it's okay, if I have no other commitments, to take a nap in the middle of the day.

Of course, she's taught me a lot about love.

She greets me enthusiastically when I return home after being out in the world, no matter how long or short I've been away. She follows me around at times as if she is interested in **everything** I do.

She shows me how happy she is when I rub her belly. She barks protectively when a strange noise can be detected in my building and is not ashamed of seeking me out or crawling into bed with me during a thunderstorm.

She can show herself as fierce or vulnerable . . .

I don't have to DO anything to win her love. Perhaps, especially when you're young, it's easy to confuse love with approval. Love is given freely from a sense of belonging together or the simple pleasure of being near someone's energy.

One doesn't deserve (or not deserve) to be loved.

But I think the biggest lesson I've learned from India has to do with the virtues of having a short-term memory and optimistic nature.

When I wake up in the morning, I'll naturally stretch out my legs. Maybe I'll turn over on my stomach and try to enjoy another few minutes of sleep, or maybe I'll roll over to a spot on my mattress where I hadn't made a recent impression.

India, who usually sleeps on the area rug at the foot of my bed, seems to know when I'm awake and not merely following a cue to move from some unspecified dream time source. When she senses I'm awake, she runs to the side of my bed.

She puts her front paws on the edge of my white sheets and balances on her hind legs. She does a sort of stutter step to keep her head, which she tilts to the side, above the top edge of my bed.

She is so excited—eager for me to pat the top of her head—and happy that I'm now going to join her in being awake. Her whole panting-stretching-dancing body seems to be saying, *Come on. Get up. Get up.*

NEW DAY

That's the greatest gift of all, to remember that any moment is a good time to start over.

Starting each day with enthusiasm, trusting that everything you might need will be provided, is no small thing.

Grateful Dozen Category: Something New, Noticing Small
Things, August 1, 2016

My Left Hand

T RUE TO FORM, WHEN I EXPERIENCED MY
SHOULDER INJURY A FEW WEEKS AGO, I TRIED
TO THINK OF WHAT I HAD TO GAIN FROM THE
EXPERIENCE.

NOT THAT I'M A POLLYANNA, BUT I THINK,
GENERALLY, THERE ARE POSITIVE LESSONS TO BE
EXTRACTED FROM ALL RANGE OF EXPERIENCES, EVEN
THE DIFFICULT ONES.

ONE OF THE FIRST THINGS I BECAME AWARE OF DURING MY RECOVERY WAS THAT I HAD TO **ASK FOR HELP.**

THIS IS NOT EASY FOR MOST PEOPLE. IT CERTAINLY HASN'T BEEN FOR ME. IT SEEMS NATURAL FOR ME TO TAKE PRIDE IN MY INDEPENDENCE. AS MANY PEOPLE DO, I'VE OFTEN EQUATED ASKING FOR HELP AS A SIGN OF WEAKNESS OR CAUSE FOR SHAME.

DESPITE ENDORSING THE IDEA THAT ACCEPTING HELP FROM OTHERS ACTUALLY SERVES THEM, I'VE HAD PROBLEMS WITH THE REALITY OF BEING IN THIS POSITION. THE IDEA OF ACCEPTING HELP IS FINE— BUT NOT SO FINE FOR **ME,** ESPECIALLY WHEN I'M UNCERTAIN HOW LONG I WILL BE IN NEED.

THE RANGE OF THINGS I FOUND MYSELF NEEDING HELP FOR SURPRISED ME. IT WAS NOT LIKE GETTING YEARLY TAX ADVICE OR NEEDING A SINGLE RIDE TO A DESTINATION. WITHOUT THE USE OF MY RIGHT ARM AND HAND, I SEEMED TO NEED HELP FOR **EVERYTHING.**

THIS LED ME TO MY NEXT LESSON.

I TRIED TO PLAN THE SIMPLE TASKS OF MY LIFE. I DID NOT JUST WANT TO AVOID WASTING TIME, I WANTED TO AVOID WASTING **OTHER PEOPLE'S** TIME,

WHEN I HAD SOMEONE COME OVER TO WALK MY DOG, I USUALLY ASKED THEM TO HELP ME WITH SOME ARM EXERCISES OR TO OPEN A CAN OR CHANGE A LIGHT BULB. ACCOMPLISH TWO GOALS WITH ONE VISIT, RIGHT?

I ALSO FELT REMINDED TO CONTEMPLATE THE PHRASE DESCRIBING PEOPLE AS HUMAN **BEINGS**, NOT HUMAN **DOINGS.** WHEN I COULDN'T PERFORM MY JOB, OR COULD ONLY DO MY JOB IN A VERY LIMITED

CAPACITY, I NEEDED TO REMEMBER NOT TO JUDGE MY WORTH BY MY PRODUCTIVITY.

I STARTED TO ACCEPT HOW CONTINUED WORK IS NEEDED IN THE AREA OF PATIENCE. AS I LOOKED AT PROSPECTS FOR REHAB, I REALIZED THAT HAVING GREATER PATIENCE IS ESPECIALLY IMPORTANT. BRINGING MY ARM BACK TO FULL FUNCTIONALITY WILL NOT BE A SHORT-LIVED VENTURE.

OPPORTUNITIES TO EXAMINE MY GROWTH HAVE BEEN IN MY FACE. MOST HAVE NOT BEEN TOTALLY UNEXPECTED, BUT I WAS SURPRISED BY A MOMENT I HAD WHEN I TRIED TO MAKE OUT THE ITEMS ON A SHOPPING LIST THE OTHER DAY.

I'M VERY RIGHT HAND DOMINANT. FORGET ABOUT SIGNING A CHECK OR CREDIT CARD SLIP WITH MY LEFT HAND.

SINCE MY INJURY, I'VE HAD TO TURN ON LIGHTS, TYPE EMAILS, BRUSH MY TEETH, AND CLEAN MYSELF AFTER GOING TO THE TOILET USING MY LEFT HAND. EVERYDAY TASKS HAVE TAKEN MUCH MORE TIME WITH THIS FORGOTTEN SIDE.

BUT NOT UNTIL I SAW MY ATTEMPTS TO WRITE A GROCERY LIST WITH MY LEFT HAND DID I REALIZE HOW MUCH JUDGMENT I HOLD AGAINST PARTS OF ME.

I PRONOUNCED THE SCRAWLED OUT LETTERS AS INEPT, JUVENILE, USELESS— **UGLY**.

EVEN AFTER ATTRIBUTING THE UNEVEN SCRIPT TO LACK OF EXPERIENCE WITH MY NON-DOMINANT HAND, I DIDN'T WANT TO THINK THE WORDS WRITTEN WITH BLACK INK ON THE BACK OF A PIECE OF PRINTER PAPER CAME FROM ME.

I GUESS I WANT TO THINK OF MYSELF IN TERMS OF

MY BEST FEATURES. I AM A GOOD WRITER AND QUICK WITH A JOKE OR OBSERVATION. I HAVE NICE LEGS. . . .
I DON'T USUALLY WANT TO ASSOCIATE MYSELF WITH WHAT'S NOT CLEVER OR ATTRACTIVE, WITH WORDS PENNED WITH MY LEFT HAND.

BUT THESE THINGS ARE PARTS OF ME, TOO. MY LEFT HAND HAS SERVED ME, THOUGH PERHAPS NOT AS EFFICIENTLY OR AS ELEGANTLY AS MY RIGHT. THESE PAST THREE WEEKS, MY LEFT HAND HAS WASHED MY DISHES, RETRIEVED COLD-PACS FROM THE FREEZER, AND TEXTED MESSAGES ON MY SMARTPHONE.

MAYBE MY HANDWRITING WITH MY LEFT HAND WILL IMPROVE SOMEWHAT AS I AM FORCED TO USE IT MORE OFTEN, BUT THAT'S NOT THE MAIN TAKEAWAY. [I DON'T EXPECT CHRISTY BROWN-LIKE ACHIEVEMENTS, THE IRISH ARTIST WITH CEREBRAL PALSY WHO DEVELOPED THE ABILITY TO TYPE AND PAINT WITH HIS LEFT FOOT.]

BUT I CAN RECOGNIZE SOME OF MY DISOWNED PARTS AS BEING IN SERVICE OF **THE WHOLE ME.**

KNOWING YOURSELF TO BE WHOLE, EVEN IF A LITTLE BROKEN, AND RECOGNIZING THAT YOUR WHOLE SELF INCLUDES ASPECTS OF YOU THAT ARE NOT PREFERRED OR NORMALLY ON DISPLAY, IS NO SMALL THING.

Grateful Dozen Category: Musings—Adventures With My Mind, Self-Appreciation, August 7, 2017

Clapping

C HICAGO'S FLAMENCO FESTIVAL. I haven't been to a
festival event in years.

    It takes place annually, usually around the end of
February or the beginning of March, when everyone is more
than tired of winter's gray skies and evenings spent watching
Netflix at home.

The festival features wonderful music and dance performed
by some of the best in the world and is sponsored by the
Cervantes Institute, an organization that promotes Spanish
language and culture.

When a couple of friends asked me to join them to see La

Chimi dance, a San Diego native currently based in Seville, I couldn't refuse.

I remembered how, years ago, when I vacationed in Spain, my partner and I caught a couple sets of gypsy style flamenco in a Sacramonte cave taverna on the outskirts of Grenada. It was a wonderful night of passionate singing, stomping, and strumming.

La Chimi (Lakshmi Basile) and ensemble of Alejandro El Gambimbas (lead singer), Bruno Serrano (singer and percussion) and Jose Manuel (guitarist) brought me back to the caves in Andalasia, even in our simple, modern setting in Chicago.

So generous and unfiltered in their passion and energy, it was obvious that they enjoyed performing, but more fundamentally, they felt connected to the music they were making. Not improvisational the same way a jazz quartet might run through *Stella by Starlight* or another classic ballad, yet they worked within a structure AND were very much *in the moment.*

After a particularly energetic series of staccato impressions the dancer made on the wood floor or a virtuoso arpeggio from the guitar, making you wonder if such a sound could be created by a man who had only five fingers on each hand (like you and me), the ensemble would shout "Joaleee!!" Ah-lay, like *olé* on steroids.

And the crowd would echo, "Joaleee!!"

My friend sitting next to me, who is much more left-brained than I am, nudged me and commented something along the lines of, "Wouldn't you love to know what they're singing?"

Rapt as I was in the performance, I didn't really care. I felt beauty in the depth of their feelings and how fully they expressed themselves, as well as how each artist respected each other. I was conscious that they wanted what they did to blend into something greater.

Curiosity came over me the next day. I looked up something about the traditions of flamenco online. I learned that there were several musical styles, some just performed by men.

I saw translations of popular lyrics. In the **Siguiriya style:**

"When I come to die, I ask of you one favor, that with the braids of your black hair they tie my hands."

I saw these words for a **tango**, "Comb your hair with my comb, for my comb is made of sugar; Whoever combs his hair with my comb, will suck his fingers."

Whether I understood the songs literally or not as they were performed, I found the singer pulling sounds out of his heart and belly, penetrating and haunting.

And the beat . . .

All night long, I thought about the clapping.

Of course, after the performance, the audience got to their feet and applauded their approval.

But clapping is such an intrinsic aspect of the art. There are rhythms and hand positions to learn, but it's an unusual sort of equalizer. In clapping, anyone can make music.

Not all people can play guitar or dance with grace and energy, but most people can clap—at least for a short period. It's one of the first things a child learns.

If just for your own pleasure, singing and clapping means everyone has an instrument to express their joy or despair, their contentment or longing.

Being able to make your own music is no small thing.

Grateful Dozen Category: Beauty, March 12, 2018

Random Gifts of Flowers

I GUESS I HAVE a strange relationship with flowers.

I can't seem to grow them on my back deck. I either under-water them or drown them. I feel inept in my abilities to arrange them. Even though they are naturally beautiful, it's hard to deny that certain people have more of a knack for putting them together.

Flowers are symbolic of things that were not right in past romantic relationships.

I remember when the young engineer I met in the French

Quarter almost thirty years ago, later to become my husband, would turn away street merchants trying to sell him a red rose to give to me, with the line, "No thanks. I'm not hungry."

Too often, it seems, people are shamed into gifting someone with flowers, and shame is never good to attach to a present.

Still, I fall under the spell of their beauty, their delicacy and ephemeral nature.

The other week, when I was walking in my neighborhood, I stopped in front of a garden on Eastwood. It was a small collection of flowers and shrubs and rocks, obviously meticulously tended. The owner of the house, a man in his seventies, I guess, wielding a special scissors, was cutting down peonies.

I felt compelled to say something. A garden so beautiful represents a lot of work. People that put in so much work in the grass and dirt make the whole neighborhood more beautiful.

"Your garden looks lovely," I said.

Snip, Snip.

"Damn, it's going to be another scorcher today. These flowers can't take the heat," he said, then added, *"You want a few?"*

I didn't even know the man's name. I couldn't imagine him giving me something, something from **his** garden, something he grew himself.

"I have to cut them all. We have quite a few in the house already."

"They are beautiful," I told him.

Snip. Snip. Snip. He handed me three and offered a little perspective. *"It's best to put odd numbers together,"* he said, and I thanked him.

I put them in one of my nicer vases as soon as I got home, and I thought about my unexpected gift.

I felt like I had a key role in the cycle of giving and receiving.

No occasion was involved. He just acted on a present

moment impulse to cut down his fragrant peonies before they browned on their stems. I think he was happy to find a new home for them, happy to find an appreciative soul for what he had to offer.

I got so much joy from smelling their sweetness and looking at them in my living room all week. I was also happy feeling that I was somehow connected to my neighbor.

I probably would not be able to pick him out in a small crowd at a local farmer's market, but displaying flowers that were given to me felt so much more gratifying than bringing home a bouquet from the grocery store.

They were planted and watched over with care and devotion.

I loved the thought that someone wanted me to have something BEAUTIFUL.

Maybe this would be a good thought to keep in my consciousness: to look for opportunities, even small ones, to share things that are pleasant to look at or inspiring.

A random gift of beauty, like a random act of kindness, is no small thing,

Grateful Dozen Category: Beauty, Surprise, June 4, 2018

Little Feet

I WAS ON THE L heading downtown for a meeting. Being after the morning commute, it was not hard to find a seat.

About two stops after I got on, a young mother, after struggling a bit to get a very expensive-looking baby buggy over the threshold of the car, navigated the carriage to a nearby spot across from me.

With one foot, she engaged the brakes and began making very exaggerated, but very loving expressions to the child in the buggy.

I couldn't see the baby's face. I assumed it was a little boy because I saw his legs in a grayish-blue and white striped onesie outfit poking out from under the awning of the cushioned cradle.

I fell in love. There is something about a child's little feet.

I remember when I had a romance with a visual artist. A friend of his, an artist himself with a reputation of accomplishment in Eastern Europe, smiled and welcomed my lover's stories of his new relationship.

He smiled and nodded. *"Yes, right now, everything is PINK,"* he said.

I suppose it's only natural that a visual artist would speak in the language of colors.

But that's how I felt about seeing this young commuter's feet. The sight made everything PINK for me, tender and promising.

I'm not normally taken to sentiment, but I was totally taken, charmed, by those tiny feet.

The baby stretched his legs upwards, without giving thought to their effect or sturdiness, without trying to use them to stand or transport him to some destination.

He was just dancing in the air. Totally absorbed by the sensation of moving his own limbs, of being able to move his limbs.

And his toes . . . it seemed like the width of his foot could barely contain the five fleshy digits. He was too young to appreciate them for the way they would help him keep his balance or kick a soccer ball or pedal a bicycle.

He still probably welcomed an adult squeezing his toes, one at a time, and repeating *This little piggy went to market . . .*

I appreciated not having a full view of the baby. Because I couldn't see a face, I didn't feel drawn to ascribe characteristics like cute, or smart, or happy. I could not say whether this child was an old soul in a very fresh form or if the child was young and innocent in every possible way.

What is it about a baby's feet?

I might look at a sadhu's feet and contemplate what kind of pilgrimages he had already walked. I might look at an old woman's feet and consider in what ways, over her lifetime, she tried to make herself fit into different shoes and perform whatever was asked of her by others.

I might look at an athlete's feet and think about how they were often overlooked in the training room while depended on in order for him to deliver on expectations.

I might look at a dancer's feet and consider how much pain and discomfort she endured because of the dancer's unwavering will.

But a baby's feet is all HOPE, an image of PURE POTENTIAL.

I like to be in the company of this kind of simple hope sometimes. To know that pure potential is nearby.

Maybe this feeling can not only be seen in an infant's feet. Maybe it can be contained in other things. It's worth recognizing anything that provides even a glimmer of hope and being with it whenever it enters your head space.

Fully taking in an image or sensation or word that lets you imbibe hope—even in a train car—is no small thing.

Grateful Dozen Category: Noticing Small Things,
Something New, September 24, 2018

A Wabi-Sabi Thanksgiving

WE LOOK FORWARD to Thanksgiving dinner. And, as we do most years, we're grateful when it's over.

There are travel delays and cooking traumas (it's easy to have problems when preparing a dinner for four times your usual crowd). And, of course, some of us experience high anxiety over political or cultural discussions breaking out over the candied cranberries.

I enjoyed conversing with the *Thanksgiving orphans* my sister invited this year, friends and acquaintances whose families live far away.

I also found special pleasure from a pre-dinner remark my

twenty-two year-old niece made, not quite a religious blessing but striking the right tone.

If you come from a place where you have more than enough, think of ways to build a longer table, not higher walls.

Oddly, the most striking thing that I recall from my family's annual food fest occupied only a few seconds. It took place after champagne and appetizers, when we were ushered into the dining room and pointed to our seats. It probably went unnoticed by most of the group.

My sister Barbara, who is an incredible cook and impeccable hostess, must have found herself with a headcount for the evening that put her in an odd position. At sixteen, our group was too small to warrant a second set of china, which she has, but was one or two too many for everyone to eat off the same Wedgwood pattern.

She decided to improvise. The subtle deviation in place settings was not lost on me.

A complete complement of Waterford crystal, for wine and water, rested above the big plate. Sterling silver rested on the starched and pressed linen tablecloth and napkin.

. . . But the fine china salad plate sat in the middle of a plain white dinner plate from her everyday collection.

My cousin Allen's wife, Marna, and I joked about the unusual place setting when we were directed to that corner of the table. At first, we acted like junior high students who didn't want to sit with the unpopular kids at the cafeteria table. **No, YOU sit there. No You. . . .**

After engaging with the idea that something was off about this place setting, it suddenly became important to me that I claim my seat behind it.

It was SO BEAUTIFUL to me, precisely because it was a little off. It consisted of mismatching parts.

It was so **WABI-SABI.**

WIKIPEDIA tells us that the origin of this aesthetic is Japanese and describes a certain type of beauty as "imperfect, impermanent, and incomplete."

The underlying, or unsaid, wonder about this is ACCEPTANCE. It's the incredible quality and nature of acceptance that makes the experience of dishes not matching or knowing that the fall flower arrangement we passed casseroles over won't last the week filled me with special appreciation.

I have been sitting at my sister's holiday tables for most of my life. Last Thursday was probably the most enjoyable Thanksgiving dinner to date.

The food is always great, but I am usually conscious of Barb wanting everything to be PERFECT, perfect in a Martha Stewart sort of way.

The meal was incredible, but I didn't feel any spirit of trying to outdo output from previous years.

This acceptance of what is and open sharing I had with the other people around the table, a feeling of being with family, even though only half of our group is related, was so beautiful.

My brother-in-law pointed out that the mismatching dinner and salad plate was a good metaphor for the gathering.

Yes, my family of birth was represented, but we also had the company of old friends, a new acquaintance of my sister's from her travel club, my late sister's husband and his second wife, her daughter and boyfriend. Conversation was easy and we all appreciated being together . . .

and it was beautiful . . .

Accepting differences and the inexplicable way things that don't match seem to go together *perfectly* is no small thing.

Grateful Dozen Category: Beauty,
November 27, 1018

See Something, Say Something

S INCE 9/11, OUR country has gotten used to a message
of fear. In a wide range of venues, everyone is asked to
be vigilant about noticing backpacks or briefcases or
shopping bags that might contain something unexpected and
nefarious.

SEE SOMETHING—SAY SOMETHING is the motto that's featured on posters in many public spaces.

I had a very different **See Something—Say Something** experience just last week. It's worth as much attention.

Last Wednesday, I was heading downtown for an afternoon matinee at the Lyric Opera. I got passes for the dress rehearsal for Cinderella (Cendrillon) as a birthday gift from my sister, Barbara.

I love going to dress rehearsals because, like me, most people in the audience are gifted their tickets from friends or family who are subscribers. They fill the beautiful, gold ceilinged auditorium with the energy of appreciation.

It snowed just a couple days earlier and then the temperature dropped dramatically. Ice was everywhere and navigating even small stretches by foot was dangerous.

When I made it to the commuter train platform to head to the Civic Opera House downtown, I remembered muttering to myself that I would not run after a train. Rather than run the risk of slipping, if a train pulled in while I was moving through the turnstile, I was prepared to just wait for the next one.

Fortunately, I didn't have to make such a decision. After stepping up to the platform, which was very much exposed to the cold and wind, I moved forward slowly to a good spot for boarding.

I noticed that the south side of the wooden platform was cleared of ice but a thick, bumpy layer of ice covered the north side of the platform.

CTA (Chicago Transit Authority) workmen, wearing their outdoor work gear and orange and yellow vests, armed with spades and small shovels, were making stabbing thrusts into the frozen side of the platform.

They were loud! The wooden platform seemed to shake underneath them, but even when a swatch of ice stubbornly refused to break down under their initial efforts, they didn't give up. They were determined to make the walkway safer for passengers to navigate.

I walked up to one workman. He didn't have snot running down his nose or anything, but he wore a look of cold discomfort and unconscious concentration. I said,

"Thank you. Thank you for breaking and clearing the ice. Thank you for making it safe for me to walk on this platform."

He blinked in surprise. Then he broke into a smile. He said, *"No one's ever thanked me for this before . . . "*

As if to get over what was close to displaying emotion, he resumed efforts with his spade, repeatedly pounding the sharp metal edge into the ice.

Jokingly, I asked him if the action was a new type of anger therapy.

He laughed. A few of his workmates came over to see what we were talking about.

I asked them if I could take a picture of them with my cell phone. I explained that I kept a blog of things I was grateful for.

As if the supper bell just rang in the firehouse, all the workers gathered around my withdrawn cell phone and started posing.

"No, no," I insisted. *"This isn't a group selfie. Go back to breaking up the ice. Pretend you're working."*

We all laughed.

We acted like we were friends. A relationship was started because I noticed something small and said THANK YOU.

Noticing an act of kindness, or extra effort, or genuine empathy, no matter how routine or outwardly insignificant—then saying that you noticed and are grateful—is no small thing.

Grateful Dozen Category: Noticing Small Things,
December 3, 2018

Friday Night Live

I TEXTED A FRIEND Thursday to see if she'd want to join me for a cocktail the following night at the Tiny Lounge. The Tiny Lounge is my absolute favorite neighborhood spot for a craft cocktail, a comfortable stool, and tasty snacks.

With uber professional and passionate bartenders (no shortcuts on ingredients allowed) and no walls of contiguous giant screen TVs, it's the antithesis of Hooters or Buffalo Wild Wings.

I knew she had just returned to Chi-town after a week-long

visit with her mother in Detroit. For her, it was a long week of getting her mother's taxes in order, cooking, shopping, and practicing detachment.

Her mom directed words of criticism at her. Even though her mother often forgot she made a harsh comment the following day, my friend was hurt as she tried very hard to listen and give her mother choices in daily matters.

For me, after starting the year with hardly any billable hours, I had to work the last three weekends. I felt I deserved some time off.

My friend responded to my text within minutes, *What time?*

I guess **Thank God it's Friday** is a universal sentiment.

Friday night is a magical time. It's a time when I'll feel free from the obligations of the workweek and not yet enmeshed in weekend household chores.

On Friday, instead of being stingy or judgmental towards myself, I'll find myself in a more forgiving and generous mood. I'll eat or drink whatever I have a yen for and feel okay about spending a little money.

Before meeting my friend at 6:00, I stopped at an ATM.

I took time to apply mascara and lipstick, which I don't normally do, but it was Friday night and I was taking myself OUT.

At 6:00, I walked off the street, up three stairs, and into the narrow room. (They don't call it TINY for nothing, I suppose.)

My friend was already sitting on a stool at the bar. She sat behind a cordial glass filled with a light, clear liquid. She was entranced by the sights and smells of Friday Night Live.

"*St. Germain*," she said, and offered me a sip. "*Smells wonderful*," she added.

She proceeded to introduce me to Jessie, the bartender. School teacher by day, bartender par excellence by night.

We watched the silhouette of his shadow flicker and dance

against the grass cloth wallpaper behind the bar. He mixed two cocktails, one in each hand, in chilled metal shakers. Like Balanchine choreography, the sight was both masculine and ethereal.

We moved to a counter-high table near the window while it was still an option. Within the next hour, the place would fill up to welcome a mixed-crowd of Friday night revelers: hipsters and middle-aged women ready to observe their own ritual.

We perused the menu which featured both snacks (when did cheese curds become a cool menu item?) and signature drinks. Variety is wonderful, but I felt compelled to stick with their *Glass Sipper*, my fav.

We drank slowly, savoring the bouquet of the lemon peel, marveling at how long the ice seemed to retain its cube shape and not melt.

While waiting for the attentive but not intrusive waitress to bring our curds and flatbread, we sipped our cocktails and toyed with our tumblers of water. And we **emptied** ourselves.

We shared our frustrations, our disappointments of the week, how we tried to keep perspective and not let things bother us; how we tried to take the high road. We talked about what we were conscious of losing sleep over and **confessed** that we hoped to sleep late the next morning.

It wasn't the alcohol's power, not directly, that felt so freeing. It was the sense of making a ***confession.***

Important to note, it was obvious that all around us, good friends were getting together to do the same. We all had come together to ***witness*** each other. We all wanted to relieve ourselves of our burdens, our disappointments and sorrows.

We were in a narrow territory, like a small island state, planted under the flag of no judgment.

Having a Friday night cocktail with a good friend—at the TINY LOUNGE—is no small thing.

Grateful Dozen Category: Neighborhood Discoveries,
Belonging, April 9, 2018

In the Ring with Greatness

ACCORDING TO PLAN, I stopped in Louisville after my first day of driving to Jonesborough, Tennessee to attend the storytelling festival. It represented a good chunk of drive time, and I thought I could take in a couple local attractions.

Of course, the Kentucky Derby Museum was a must. I also planned on visiting a distillery along the bourbon or whiskey trail on my way to Knoxville where I planned to stay the following night.

I sampled some excellent Kentucky style *hot chicken* at

Royal's for dinner and caught a set of jazz at Jimmy Can't Dance, an unexpected find—a basement bar and music venue downtown.

While walking down Main Street near Seventh, I saw signs for the Ali Center, a tribute to Muhammad Ali who was from Louisville, and visiting before I left town the following day became fixed in my mind.

What a wonderful museum!

It had something for everyone: for sports enthusiasts, for spiritual seekers, for fans of spoken word art (with phrases like, "Float like a butterfly, sting like a bee," maybe Ali was the father of rap) for twentieth century history buffs, and for supporters of social justice.

Ali was a role model in so many ways. His life and authenticity is inspiring.

Throughout the museum and gift shop, a big emphasis was made of **Red Bike Moments**.

At the age of twelve, Cassius Marcellus Clay Jr.'s red Schwinn bicycle was stolen from outside his Louisville home. He found a policeman and confessed that he wanted to *whup* the thief.

The policeman turned out to be a boxing coach. He helped the young Clay channel his anger and frustration into a commitment to excellence at his sport.

After he started developing a reputation, the young Clay quickly came to the understanding that he could use his position as heralded athlete and brash personality to better the lives of others.

His **red bike moment,** his point of transformation, revolved around taking a devastating experience and turning it into a personnel pledge to always do his best and to be of service to others.

Front pages from newspapers decorated the walls of the museum. In small alcoves, video clips of famous and famously funny interviews with the likes of Howard Cosell ran in perpetual loops.

Larger-than-life posters and three-dimensional timelines brought us through his personal history; through unforgettable bouts and audacious quips, through his legal battles and public backlash over his decision not to serve in the military, through adopting Islam and changing his name, and his world travels as an ambassador of sorts after his boxing career ended.

The museum featured a variety of interactive exhibits.

My favorite was a chance to shadow box in the ring with him. I snapped a photo on my cell phone and sent it to a friend with the caption, "He didn't land a blow."

But I changed for having gotten in the ring with his likeness.

Oh my God. His silhouette was unmistakable. Lean and muscular and fast . . . . Ducking and weaving. Dancing. I felt so clunky and slow in comparison. He was the epitome of grace in action.

Our time circling each other in virtual reality only served to bring his spirit deeper into my heart—a symbol of what I'd like all people to do for each other. Set a good example of truth and determination.

He spoke his truth. He was prepared to accept the consequences of his decisions and actions. He was in touch with his humanity during every chapter of his life. He embodied the dignity of the individual because he never lost sight of how he was connected to the fabric of life.

Understanding that greatness is not marked by trophies so much as by **commitment** is no small thing.

Grateful Dozen Category: People Who Touch Me,
October 15, 2018

Infinite Variety

I WENT TO MY neighborhood grocery store the other day. I try to shop local whenever I can.

The store is fairly small (the parking lot holds less than thirty cars) but it always amazes me how well they satisfy the tastes of such an ethnically and culturally diverse clientele.

While not specifically on my shopping list, I found myself lingering at their floor-to-ceiling display of HONEY.

Oh my God. There were so many different kinds.

There are different types of honey based on source, such as

clover or wildflower or eucalyptus or alfalfa or buckwheat or orange blossom.

Honey can also be categorized by grade, reflecting color and water content, or by process. There is raw and pasteurized, filtered and strained.

When I looked at the jars and labels in the display, I also sensed a sort of boutique identification customers might have with certain brands.

In the honey world, small batch is cool. Limited distribution rules. I'm sure some aficionados look for honey manufactured by old hippies living in communes in Michigan or prepared at an Amish farm and carted off by horse-drawn wagon (eventually to be delivered by a diesel-powered truck to a grocery store).

Other types of the sweet golden condiment boast of an ethnic heritage and the foods they are best suited for. For example, there are brands that are purchased specifically for Greek or Mexican or Indian desserts.

Mostly contained in fancy glass jars, indicating purity, packaging for honey has come a long way since the days of plastic Pooh-Bear squeeze bottles.

Friday night, I joined several friends for a movie and a pizza. We went to a pizzeria by the theater where none of us had been before. It featured *coal-fired* pizza.

In Chicago, a town with a longstanding pizza tradition, I thought I had sampled every type of pizza there was.

I had favorite spots for thin or pan or stuffed. I could feast on vegetarian or meaty. I even have sampled pizza with caramelized cheese edges, but coal-fired was new to me.

With extra fresh herbs and spices, it turned out to be very good. We all wanted to come back and try other combinations of ingredients.

Infinite variety makes me think about infinite possibilities.

These days, I've been getting upset over people who are afraid of immigrants, afraid of anything that's different. They're very easy prey for politicians or media personalities to stir up fear in them.

They probably don't think much about the lesson of multi-tiered shelves of honey (or cereal or chips) at their grocery store. They probably are numb to getting a similar lesson when they take a walk.

There's an incredible *variety* of things, of grasses and leaves and animals, in nature.

Infinite variety leads to infinite possibilities.

I know that I want to live my life believing in possibilities.

Except for different strains of Ebola viruses, infinite possibilities is usually a good thing.

I am glad my mind is tuned up to notice these kinds of lessons all the time. Living with an open and inquisitive mind leads me to make conscious and informed choices all the time regarding how I want to live going forward.

Seeing lessons in the simple activities of daily life is no small thing.

Grateful Dozen Category: Musings—Adventures with My Mind, Neighborhood Discoveries, January 5, 2019

Everyone Needs A Hero

A S A COMBINED birthday/Christmas present, my friend Holly gave me a Ruth Bader Ginsburg *action figure*.

After seeing the recent documentary and watching special news segments about her, I have found myself in awe of her bravery, intellect, and tenacity.

Although an important public figure of rare status, only nine people hold the same job at the same time, I admit to being surprised by her recent popularity, earning her the nickname, **the Notorious RBG.**

Looking at the boxed collectible, her likeness as a doll decked out in her judge's black robe and jabot (white lace collar), sporting her unmistakable dark-framed eyeglasses, with a gavel, as an accessory in a plastic bubble nearby, I have to laugh.

As I hosted a family gathering Christmas Eve, I displayed my RBG action figure in a prominent place on my bar, near a blooming poinsettia.

Everyone who saw it smiled or laughed out loud. We shared comments about what we found special or amazing about her.

Who would think that an eighty-five-year-old woman from Brooklyn with a quiet voice and respectful style of communicating, a mother and grandmother, an opera lover, would be such a rock star?

Yes, she survived several bouts of cancer, the loss of her soul mate, and more than a few POTUS tweets disparaging her ability to continue in her role on the bench as she ages, but those facts are merely footnotes in a bio that's still being written.

When I contemplate her life and why she is so inspirational to me, I can say that I'm impressed with:

- How she lives guided by her values.

- Her dry sense of humor.

- Her thoughtfulness in speech and actions.

- Her ability to discuss things objectively with people she disagrees with.

- Her bravery in speaking the truth and her clarity of understanding, taking on the important task of writing dissenting opinions as well as majority opinions, knowing that getting an argument on the record is important to history even when a short-term outcome has been lost.

- Giving 110% to everything she does.

She stood out in college and law school as having a sharp legal mind, but her reputation was not just built on academic excellence. She took action.

The victim of discrimination herself, she became an advocate and champion of the idea that it is good for the individuals concerned and good for society that all people can reach their potential.

I suppose she's a hero to me because she embodies some things that I don't think I could ever accomplish.

She's made law and advocacy her life's work and, already spanning decades, doesn't plan on retiring or slowing down. In my eighties, I think that stamping my passport with different destinations will be my main preoccupation.

She's also a hero, I suppose, because there are many examples I can take from how she's chosen to live her life that I can integrate into how I want to live mine.

She's a champion of **incremental victories.**

Some of this is the nature of law and culture.

Issues come up for debate based on specific cases. Not every dispute becomes a landmark case, but every big decision comes out of the series of preceding decisions and arguments.

There are winners and losers of cases, conservative and more progressive interpretations of the law, but history cannot go backwards.

I am inspired by the Notorious RBG. She is so different, but not completely unlike me. I look to her as an example of how to become a hero to myself.

There will always be unpredictable events that spark unanticipated changes, but so much happens because people simply show up every day and do their job; because they are willing to build on incremental victories.

With or without a gavel, giving voice to your values and focusing on what's in front of you right now, appreciating all the things that allow you to move one step further in the right direction, is no small thing.

Grateful Dozen Category: What so Funny? People Who Touch Me, January 7, 2019

She Called Me Hon

I LOVE TO EAT breakfast out.

It's a small, affordable indulgence. Besides, the host doesn't greet you as if you are a leper when you announce wanting a table for one.

Neighborhood spots for breakfast are wonderful discoveries; the product of a friend's recommendation or the recollection of seeing a sign when you are driving or walking close to home.

Breakfast spots usually have specialties, so intentions for

return trips are filed in your brain immediately after your first experience.

When you have a hankering for perfectly golden brown waffles (which you can't make at home), or a particular type of ethnic-themed skillet, or a special Benedict with **real** hollandaise, you know exactly where to go.

Besides, there is nothing like having breakfast with your neighbors to make you feel like you are part of a community.

Glen, my designated driver for my recent trip to the oral surgeon, remarked on Alps Pancake House as we passed it en route to my morning appointment. He said it was a good place for breakfast.

It didn't take me long to decide to check it out for myself.

A family-owned establishment, it was a wonderful throwback to an earlier time.

It was busy, but I did not have to wait for a seat at a booth or table.

Alps is wonderfully **un-trendy.** They didn't boast serving Intelligentsia or a premium brand of fair trade coffee and my request for decaffeinated tea did not lead to options. It simply meant *Lipton.*

Still, the host seemed happy to direct me to a small booth. Water was brought to my table right away as I was given an extensive, photo-rich spiral bound menu to peruse.

Their waitresses were career servers, mostly single mothers I imagined, and not actresses who chose breakfast restaurant work because it is not disruptive of other pursuits.

My waitress, a bleach-blond forty-something, approached my booth within moments of me pulling my coat off.

"Do you want coffee, hon? Do you want more time?"

After I studied my menu options, I ordered French toast and settled in to observe simple bits of neighborhood life taking place around me.

I also took relish in checking out the standard diner condiments that occupied every table.

Every table had a bowl of circular styrene single-serve containers of pure whipped butter, another bowl of similarly shaped half and half containers, a chrome rack featuring an assortment of jellies, glass salt and pepper shakers, a chrome-topped sugar dispenser, and an unrecognizable brand of Louisiana-style hot sauce.

Each table also sported a little plastic dish of every possible sugar substitute a customer could possibly want, all color coded; pink packets of Sweet 'n Low, blue packets of Equal, and yellow packets of Splenda.

Five minutes after my breakfast platter was brought to me, my waitress checked in.

"How you doing, hon?"

I loved the diversity of the clientele.

There were several hispanic men, I'd guess in their early thirties, sitting along the counter, wearing heavy white socks and gym shoes, consuming big breakfasts and taking advantage of endless coffee refills. They appeared to be getting ready for weekend side jobs in construction.

At a nearby table, I spotted a Middle-Eastern girl, probably a student at the nearby junior college, out with her friends, descendants of European immigrants.

Her thick black hair was covered by a mauve hijab, only exposing wavy wisps by her ears. She wore a dark green, long sleeved tee, probably a school color, and jeans. Except for her head scarf, she looked exactly like her classmates.

There was a middle-aged black couple with their teenage daughter sitting at a table nearby. The girl wore a rhinestone tiara (from *Party City*, no doubt) to celebrate her birthday.

When their waitress brought a candle-topped confection

to their table and started singing Happy Birthday, the whole restaurant joined in.

When I experience such ease and openness about sharing breakfast with neighbors that I don't know by name, it's hard for me to imagine building concrete walls between people who have so much to share.

Being served extra thick French toast by a woman, not a relative, who calls you *Hon* is no small thing.

Grateful Dozen Category; Belonging, Neighborhood Discoveries,
March 4, 2019

But Seriously,
What so Funny?

R ECENTLY, A FACEBOOK friend (someone I mean to talk to more often but rarely do) posted a link on her timeline. The link led me to a compilation of inspirational slogans, some *poster-ized* with complementary graphic, some attributed to writers or motivational speakers, some not.

- **Most of the shadows of this life are caused by us standing in our own sunshine.**

- **Good times make wishbones. Hard times make backbones.**

- **You wanna know the difference between a master and a beginner? The master has failed more times than the beginner has ever tried.** (These words are displayed with a rendering of Yoda from Star Wars.)

All these quotes seem like they could jump off the walls of a therapist's waiting room.

Don't get me wrong, I'm all for inspiration, but seriously . . .

I guess I take issue with some of these slogans simply because they are over-used. The first time I read "Sing like no one is listening. Love like you've never been hurt. Dance like nobody's watching," it moved me close to tears.

After the hundredth exposure, I've found myself close to tears for a totally different reason.

And the proverb, "If life gives you lemons, make lemonade," I've heard the expression so often, instead of lemonade, I'd sooner reach for a stronger beverage.

I don't like reductionism as a general rule. I understand the motivation to crystallize a sentiment into a short, pithy phrase, but often, these little adages can't capture the complexity of their subject, and throwing out a catchy phrase allows people to refrain from trying to discern and communicate something that has multiple layers—a worthy pursuit in my book.

I don't like emojis for a similar reason. Too many people use them instead of trying to understand and communicate their own feelings.

Some sayings poke fun at the effort to capture things in a simple phrase and I appreciate the impulse behind them. As an example, the saying "Philosophers are people who tell other people, that are much happier than they are, how to live," makes me laugh.

But so many sayings, while well-intentioned in their use, just get something wrong that is critical to understanding. Things are often taken out of context.

In *Hamlet*, Polonius's parting advice to his son, "To thine own self be true," has long been taken as an example of profundity. In actuality, within the context of the play, this adage is meant as a trite saying from a doddering old man who fancies himself the dispenser of all things wise.

"Keep calm and carry on" has been embraced as a tongue 'n cheek phrase for moving forward despite challenges. It actually originated in Britain's Ministry of Information during World War II as morale boosting propaganda. It was not used, as intended, at the time.

After putting out a short series of other stoic aphorisms, this catch phrase never found its way to London's subway stations or shop windows. It was meant to be used **only** in the event of Germany actually invading British soil.

When I was in my twenties, I liked to use phrases that sounded deep but were, at their core, absurd.

To puzzled faces, I'd toss out, "Just because something is obvious doesn't mean it's <u>not</u> true," or "There are two kinds of people in the world; those who put people into two kinds and those who don't."

But seriously, let's all lighten up!

After a workday, where I might have rearranged a lot of appointments in my Outlook calendar or spent an hour in a conference room decorated with framed posters depicting men involved in extreme sports like mountain-climbing, or white-water rafting, featuring a single-word headline like ATTITUDE or TEAMWORK, I like to have a cocktail.

At home, I'll take out a favorite spirit or pour a glass of Syrah and place my cocktail on my ***Confucius*** coaster, the one that says **I never said all that shit,** and I'll smile.

Surrounding yourself with little things that make you laugh is no small thing.

Grateful Dozen Category: What's So Funny,
March 25, 2019

Hearts and Minds

MY FRIEND SUSAN, who lives in Arizona, sent me an email recently about sending my dad's army patches back to me. I got them two days ago.

I pretty much had forgotten about them and about how they came into her possession, but they must have re-surfaced among her things and returning them to me was something she wanted to do.

Some years ago, I was scraping to make ends meet. All too

familiar with that situation, my friend had created several ways to generate extra money. She transcribed cassette tapes for wannabe authors and she sold things on eBay.

I thought she might be able to turn these WWII relics into cash by auctioning them off to a collector. I'm not exactly sure how I ended up with them—how they didn't end up in one of my sisters' basements.

I don't know much about the years of my father's service. Not unusual for the time, I hear. He didn't talk about his experience.

From what I understand, my father was drafted, cutting short his plans to pursue a career in law.

He was trained to be a medic and shipped off to serve in the Philippines. He saw awful things that I can't even imagine. He saw too many young men torn apart. Being charged with trying to put them back together took a toll on him.

He was awarded a purple heart. I don't know the details about a specific incident or battle.

It became a joke, of sorts, in our household. Whenever me or one of my sisters was unhappy about something or felt cheated by the institutions or authorities that imposed rules on our lives, my dad would offer to fetch his medal from his top bureau drawer.

He'd feign sympathy and say . . .

"Oh, that's too bad. Do you want my purple heart?"

They were referred to as the **greatest generation.** I don't know if they had much choice. They did their best in the situations they found themselves in.

I got wistful while looking at my father's army patches after slipping them out of the small bubble wrap reinforced envelope in which they crossed the country.

He achieved the rank of tech sergeant and returned to Chicago after his tour of duty. He lived with his parents, got into his father's business, then met my mother. He didn't go on to law school.

His acts of bravery were not over once he came back to Illinois. He had job disappointments and health issues. He lost a child in a car accident. He had money and legal issues to deal with, based on associations, not because of personal failings.

In other words, he had to endure all sorts of challenges, like people often do. He did his best.

I had to think about where my mind was at when I packaged these family keepsakes to see if my friend could sell them for me. I didn't have much cash and the thought of asking my mother for financial help, which I had done many times, was painful.

I don't think Susan could figure out a way to package these mementos for sale, or maybe she didn't want to sell them. I'm not sure why, but they stayed in Arizona for years. What would they have been worth to someone?

I realized how difficult some choices are when you're strapped for money. I have given a lot of thought lately to the hundreds of thousands of federal employees who are living without paychecks now (because of the government shutdown).

Many family members are taking on part-time jobs. Many, who have been self-sufficient most of their lives, have been forced to ask their parents or neighbors or children for help.

People have had to choose between food and medicine, or have had to postpone mortgage payments or paying off a school expense.

Others are looking through their possessions and deciding what they can part with that would be of value to someone else.

All these people—everyone who has had to make a hard choice, everyone who wants to work but finds limited opportunities, everyone who tries to take care of his needs and advocate for himself and others, everyone who tries to do his best—touch me. I'm grateful for the examples of their lives.

They all deserve purple hearts.

Knowing that life is a gift but that living takes courage is no small thing.

Grateful Dozen Category: People Who Touch me, Musings— Adventures With My Mind, January 21, 2019

Safe Passage

My Cuisinart finally gave up. (When I first got my food processor, they didn't make mixers and toasters and other things, so to me, the term *Cuisinart* is synonymous with food processor.)

After many years of service, a little electrical tape around one spot of exposed cord, countless hand washings of the blade, and months of pulse only operation, I recognized it was time to put her down.

I got my Cuisinart food processor, like many, as a wedding

present. It was the early eighties. It was after the fondue pot craze and before counter-sized espresso machines became the rage.

Needless to say, this go-to kitchen device lasted about ten times longer than my marriage. (Not sure what the lesson is in that. Always ask for a warranty?)

So, I finally trekked to B3 (Bed, Bath & Beyond) with the half dozen coupons I've received in the mail since Christmas.

A nine-cup model was on sale, although not on the floor. They offered to ship one—no charge—to my home, estimating delivery to be about a week. Perfect.

True enough, the box was delivered as promised.

I ripped open the outer packaging. The branded box fit exactly into the labeled, and well-taped, brown corrugated shell. (Obviously, the B3 shipping department, having to pay UPS based on circumference, had a lot of experience with this.)

As I pulled a molded cardboard tray out, I had to marvel at the attention given to the packaging.

The molded cardboard seemed especially cushiony, like oatmeal paper on steroids. Spaces were notched out to hold the separate components: the base which housed the motor, the plastic cylinder, and the cover that has to lock in place before the motor can engage.

The blade was wrapped in a heavy-duty plastic skin and nestled carefully inside the main vessel. Any component that could be scratched or marred, wore a plastic bag, which was printed with a warning not to place it over anyone's head.

This cautionary instruction seemed so obvious, I found myself laughing. I can't imagine it being necessary. Still, I decided it was good that someone takes the time and care to include it.

Safety in all things, right?

The last Monday of January has become a small day of

celebration to anyone who sends or receives things. It's *Bubble Wrap Appreciation Day.* I was surprised when I first found out about the observance.

I recognize that using bubble wrap has gone into disfavor for ecological reasons. For years, it delighted me when I would receive a package and get to pop the bubbles after all the parts were removed from the box.

Pop-pop-pop.

There was a childish glee I experienced when unrolling sheets of bubble wrap, but there is another aspect to appreciating protective packaging.

As a culture, we value things that are new. Whether a new toy or electronic device purchased online, packaged in layers of bubble wrap and Styrofoam peanuts, or a new car, transported cross-country on specially designed trucks.

The ultimate example of newness is a baby.

A new being, before birth, travels for months encapsulated in amniotic fluid in its own membrane.

Safe. Valued. Cherished.

When I think about my car, which is well over five years old. I have to acknowledge that I will travel for months with dry cleaner receipts tucked away in the visor and fast food napkins on the floor mat.

When I consider my clothes or dishes, as I own them longer, I expect them to get stains or cracks. As a possession ages, I'll give less and less care to their condition and use.

When something is NEW, I tend to treat it with more reverence. I don't think I'm alone here.

I suppose all things degrade over time, but there's a special honeymoon period when something is new. I think new things are treated with extra care.

I looked at the well-designed packaging for my new food processor. I am grateful for the quality of molded cardboard and the extra plastic bags. I wish all things had good protection in their journeys—over their whole lifetimes.

For me, as I go through my life, protection might involve a community of friends or like-minded people to spend time with, or maybe a guaranteed income, or basic healthcare.

We all need some level of protection.

Treating everything like it's new, like everything is worthy of safe passage, is no small thing.

Grateful Dozen Category: Musings—Adventures With My Mind, January 28, 2019

The Fine Art of Silliness

WHEN I WAS growing up and my mother wanted to introduce discipline into my life without being heavy-handed or sanctimonious, she liked re-telling an old joke.

So there was this couple, tourists from the Midwest, taking in the sights of the Big Apple, when they came across a beatnik or Bohemian along Seventh Avenue. (Remember, this was the sixties, and we had different names for street people.)

"Excuse us, young man," they said. "Could you tell us how to get to Carnegie Hall?"

The man had a simple reply.

"Practice, man. Practice."

Oddly enough, I remembered this quip as I took in one of the most unusual concerts I've ever attended.

Saturday night, a friend had me meet her at a suburban church to hear a rare performance by the St. Luke's Bottle Band.

Their penchant for schtick—old-fashioned, over-the-top humor—couldn't disguise the fact that they were good musicians and well-rehearsed. That they took the silliness of their art quite seriously led to a very enjoyable evening.

They held a series of concerts to celebrate forty years as a group, and, as you might guess, their instruments were mostly beer bottles, filled to different levels to create variations in pitch.

Different sections of the group would either blow, strike, or pluck their bottles to create different sounds.

I knew I was in for a vastly different kind of show when I took my seat in the church's second floor auditorium, probably the site for Sunday School plays or maybe book lectures on social justice and Christian teachings.

I saw the musicians PARADE from the back of the auditorium to places onstage where three levels of long covered tables with more bottles waited for them.

The players wore playful costumes, from bright green sequined sheaths and feather boas to Hawaiian shirts and hunting hats.

Many carried their instruments with them, which amounted to six-packs of half to near-empty brown Leinenkugel bottles (a favorite workingman's import from Chippewa Falls, Wisconsin).

Yes, indeedy. I wonder what Jesus would say.

Under the guidance of Maestro Paul Phillips, who started the group before the Reagan administration, the St.Luke's Bottle Band performed a surprisingly wide selection: from classical melodies (like Brahms' lullaby and Bizet's Farandole), to bastardized Beatles songs and familiar folk tunes.

The ensemble of pluckers and blowers were filled out with a fiddler, a bagpipe player, and a few other instrumentalists. Some had pretty good voices, too, which were featured on several numbers.

Their comedic timing was spot-on. Before each piece, Maestro Phillips would coax a laugh from the audience by raising his baton in a very dramatic way, as if he was conducting a world class orchestra, not an Over-the-Hill gang wielding mostly empty beer bottles.

Between selections, he offered bits of the group's history, and, as an ongoing enterprise of forty years, outlasting most marriages and the tenures of countless pastors, their longevity was something they could be proud of.

Their five minutes of fame came in 1996 (I believe) when they performed a Christmas medley on the *David Letterman Show*. They also appeared on *America's Got Talent* many years later.

Except for these once in a decade TV appearances, their state-of-the-art wackiness has not made them a household name. That sort of intrigues me and adds to the wonder of what they do.

There's an old adage about dancing like there's no one watching. In seeing the St. Luke's Bottle Band exhibit their collective musical talent and comedic chops, I recognize that what they do together takes repetition. (God knows what they have to do to get their bottles to play in pitch.)

I have to wonder what it's like to practice when shows are so rare. Except for every-other-year-performances at the church and striking, blowing, and popping once a decade on TV, they don't seem to have regularly advertised dates.

But I like this idea—that practicing in order to get better or to do something with greater ease, is complemented by enjoying the company of others also interested in conscious repetition.

I decided I'd love to be a fly on the wall, or fellow blower, in rehearsals. I imagine they have a hoot!

So, my mind comes back to my mother's quip, "How do you get to Carnegie Hall? Practice, man. Practice."

For all of us, a well-lived life is largely in the way we PRACTICE. It's the little things we attend to that prepare us for the big moments.

Practicing, and exhibiting, the fine art of silliness is no small thing.

Grateful Dozen Category: Musings—Adventures With My Mind, What's so Funny? June 11, 2019

Inner Beauty

O N A RECENT Sunday, I went with a friend to an audio consultant's storefront for an informal concert.

With seating for about thirty, this type of intimate *salon* is a great way to experience music. In addition to fine musicians, often very talented music majors from DePaul and other nearby universities, the owner of Pro Musica is a sound engineer and the mix is impeccable.

Featured were two violinists and a pianist playing classical works that were unfamiliar to me. (Per my short post-concert conversation with them, I learned that there were not many pieces written for this combination of instruments.)

Even though the violinists were more visible during the concert, standing on separate wooden platforms around eight feet apart, I was really taken by the pianist.

The thin young man on the bench had black hair and a very engaged, but not overly serious, demeanor. Although he had sheets of music splayed out in front of him, he didn't seem to get lost in the paper. He was well-rehearsed and seemed at ease.

Besides, the piano sounded wonderful!

I observed Ken, the host for the occasion, talking to regular concert attendees during intermission.

I seem to recall him explaining that the piano was a 1928 Steinway, but—he bragged—he had all the ACTION replaced within the past year.

Certainly, I knew that Steinway was a higher-end brand. I've seen Steinway grands in concert halls and in movies, in bio-pics of important pianists. Glenn Gould, famously eccentric and other-worldly talented, supposedly insisted on only playing on a Steinway.

A Steinway grand can be up to nine feet in length and, featuring an iron frame, can be significantly heavier than most other brands. With shiny black mahogany finish, an open or closed lid, setting apart from a full orchestra or alone on a stage, it can look quite imposing.

People, myself included, can be very impressed with the silhouette of a grand piano. For the most part, when I think of a piano, my mind conjures up the image of this sensual, this curved piece of dark wood.

Its black and white keys are so precious that they have to be covered when not in use. A grand piano is so majestic and worthy of respect that anyone who plays it has to sit down before it. A person's hands cannot command their complete range of eighty-eight keys, nor work the pedals, while standing.

But I had to take in Ken's comments really deeply . . . Most people think of a piano as a PIECE OF FURNITURE. To really appreciate the instrument, you need to think about the **action**, the mechanism by which sound is created.

When a key is pressed, things are set in motion for a felt-covered hammer to hit a string. In a Steinway piano, apparently, these hammers are mounted to the body of the instrument, not to the keys. I guess this can make for a bigger sound.

As I left Pro Musica, after the Sunday afternoon concert, I felt compelled to look INTO the open lid of the grand, not to just see it as a piece of furniture.

There's an old saying about beauty being in the *eye of the beholder*. I suppose this is true of many things. Beauty is subjective.

Different people find different things beautiful and have different preferences. Some men like slim women. Others like curvy women. Some people enjoy the view of a city skyline at dusk, and others swoon over a view of the ocean at sunrise.

But inner beauty is different. Inner beauty is less about the object of beauty and more about the one who sees the beauty in something.

A person who can see the inner beauty of a piano or a painting or another person has committed time and thought to understanding how that thing works or how a person ticks, what makes it special.

Inner beauty is about a person cultivating the capacity to appreciate what they experience.

Once this ability is understood and nurtured in one area of life, perhaps the unique way a key activates a hammer that plucks a string within a piano's body, seeking out the inner beauty, the distinctive nature of anything, can be applied to everything.

Looking under the lid of a piano and trying to understand how it makes sound is no small thing.

Grateful Dozen Category:
Musings—Adventures with My Mind, Beauty,
May 27, 2019

About the Author

Returning to her hometown in 2008, after nearly one year spent, unsuccessfully, trying to create a new career in a new town, Deborah Hawkins found herself fighting depression and struggling to maintain solvency. In her early fifties, looking for financial help from her family was especially hard. A car accident, caused by an uninsured driver, kept her off her feet for months. She felt cursed.

She began blogging on gratitude in 2010 as a way to focus on positives and elevate her mood. Inspired by Eckhart Tolle's words, "Acknowledging the good that is already in your life is the foundation for all abundance," she developed a mindfulness orientation for her own gratitude practice. This practice led her to post weekly over the last decade; around 500 posts.

Beyond traditional gratitude journals and lists, Deborah's approach focuses on understanding things that sparked gratitude in past experiences and using this understanding to identify similar qualities in new situations. She attributes her gratitude practice with bringing a sense of empowerment and contentment to her life.

She plans to make her process available as a teleseminar in the near future. Deborah has a BA from Knox College and lives in Chicago.